Criminal Justice
Recent Scholarship

Edited by
Marilyn McShane and Frank P. Williams III

A Series from LFB Scholarly

Prison Rape
Law, Media, and Meaning

Michael A. Smyth

LFB Scholarly Publishing LLC
El Paso 2011

Library of Congress Cataloging-in-Publication Data

Smyth, Michael A., 1951-
  Prison rape : law, media, and meaning / Michael A. Smyth.
    p. cm. -- (Criminal justice: recent scholarship)
  Includes bibliographical references and index.
  ISBN 978-1-59332-474-2 (hbk. : alk. paper)
  1. Prisoners--Sexual behavior--United States. 2. Male rape--United
States. 3. Sex crimes--United States. 4. Prison violence--United
States. 5. Prison administration--United States. 6. Prisons in mass
media--United States. I. Title.
  HV8836.S69 2011
  365'.643--dc23
                                        2011021129

ISBN 978-1-59332-474-2

Printed on acid-free 250-year-life paper.

Manufactured in the United States of America.

Table of Contents

CHAPTER ONE

Introduction

In prisons and jails throughout the nation, "[b]oys are prostituted to the lust of old convicts. Nature and humanity cry aloud for redemption from this dreadful degradation," Rev. Dwight's report lamented. A Christian missionary and one of this country's first prison reformers, Rev. Dwight founded the Boston Prison Discipline Society in 1825. The following year, he authored the first in what would be a series of 29 annual reports to the organization on the condition of prisons and inmates in the United States, a document generally believed to contain the first mention of prison rape published on this continent. In that forum, Rev. Dwight asserted, "There can be but one sufficient excuse for Christians suffering such evils to exist in prisons in this country as do exist; and that is, that they are not acquainted with the real state of things. When I shall bring before the Church of Christ a statement of what my eyes have seen," he declared, "there will be a united and powerful effort to alleviate the miseries of Prisons."[1]

Notwithstanding Rev. Dwight's urgent proclamation some 177 years earlier, it was not until 2003 that President George W. Bush affirmed efforts to define prison rape as a critical social issue when he signed into law the Prison Rape Elimination Act (PREA). Initially introduced to the legislature the preceding year as the Prison Rape Reduction Act, in the spring of 2003 the more ambitiously titled Prison Rape Elimination Act sailed swiftly and virtually uncontested through the 108th Congress on a tide of strikingly bipartisan support. The final vote favoring passage of the new law was unanimous in both the House of Representatives and in the Senate.

Despite the fact that the Prison Rape Elimination Act neither created a new category of criminal behavior nor provided a new cause

1

of action for prisoners if and when they should become victims of sexual assault, the new law was widely heralded as a major breakthrough, particularly as it served to bring "prison's dirty secrets" out of the closet.[2] For example, Lara Stemple, former Executive Director of Stop Prisoner Rape, remarked, "'The passage of this law is a major milestone, finally bringing prisoner rape out of the shadows.'"[3] Like Stemple, Wendy McElroy of Fox News commented on the importance of the PREA as a means to "a bright light...on an almost unseen social problem."[4] Implied in such statements is the notion that heretofore knowledge of prison rape had largely been confined behind the reticent walls of the institutions where it occurs. This same idea is echoed in the text of the PREA, which states, "Members of the public and government officials are largely unaware of the epidemic character of prison rape and the day-to-day horror experienced by victimized inmates."[5]

In light of its seemingly frequent representation in the news media, in legal discourse, as well as a variety of other social locations, including day-to-day talk among individuals, do such statements accurately reflect the extent of knowledge about prison rape outside prison walls? In fact, they may not. Indeed, it may be that prison rape has long been a widely known and commonly acknowledged part of carceral life in the United States. It may be that, as Fleisher (2005) contends, prison rape is:

> an idea that's shared by inmates in American prisons and community citizens. The idea of prison rape stretches from urban neighborhoods and rural communities, to schools and mega-plex theatres, to television and books and newspaper articles, to the rich and poor, to the old and young, to jails and prison, and even to the halls of the highest levels of state and federal government.[6]

Taking Fleisher's assertion seriously, this research relies on archival data and employs content analysis to explore and map the field of thought about prison rape in two particular arenas of public discourse, the print news media and appellate court opinions. Understanding representations of the phenomenon as specific symbols, stories, and worldviews used to interpret and respond to prisoner rape, a number of primary and related questions are addressed in order to map the field of thought about the subject in these particular arenas of meaning making. For example, what is the relationship among the various constructions articulated within and across these locations over time? Do they indicate contestation over the meaning of prison rape? Or might they be understood as mutually constitutive? Alternatively, are they simply parallel-running discourses that remain disconnected from one another? How and to what extent have various constructions of "prison rape" and the relationships among them changed over time? Collectively, the answers to these questions yield an empirical portrait of the phenomenon as it has been understood within and across two important arenas of meaning making. Relying on the findings from the empirical analyses, an analytic discussion is developed aimed at theorizing the field of thought about sexual violence and state punishment[7].

THEORETICAL CONCERNS

At the broadest level, this research can be located within the sociology of punishment, a field that has been described as "a tradition of thinking about punishment...differing from penology and the philosophy of punishment."[8] Scholars in the latter fields focus on questions related to the effectiveness of punishment or its moral justification, respectively. In contrast, scholars of the sociology of punishment—while not denying that penal mechanisms are primarily geared toward crime control and are shaped by that end—nonetheless argue that punishment cannot be understood entirely in those terms. Instead, punishment must be understood as an institution shaped by historical tradition and cultural style. To the extent that penal institutions are oriented toward problems of crime control, they do so in a manner mediated by "cultural conventions, economic resources, institutional dynamics, and political arguments."[9] Garland (1991) asserts that there are practical advantages to be gained from this perspective:

> Potentially, at least, it offers to provide an informed, empirical basis for understanding the ways in which penal systems actually operate in modern society and can thus help to develop more realistic expectations and objectives for penal

policy and more appropriate strategies for putting policies into effect (e.g. Downes 1988). [T]he conventional "penological" and "philosophical" approaches both base themselves on an implicit—and rather badly worked out—sociology of punishment, insofar as they rely on certain commonsense conceptions of what kind of institution punishment is and what kinds of social purposes it serves. To undertake a sociological analysis of punishment is thus to reinspect the basic presumptions made about punishment rather than simply to take them on trust.[10]

In the mid-1970's a surge of interest in the sociology of punishment followed the publication of Foucault's *Discipline and Punish: the Birth of the Prison.*[11] To a great extent, this was due to Foucault's demonstration to a broad audience of sociologists and historians the far-reaching social significance of punishment and the sort of fundamental insights to be gained from research focusing on it. At the same time, Foucault's work very much connected with the theoretical and ideological concerns of scholars who had already begun to develop a skeptical critique of modern criminalizing processes.[12] From the 1970's until the early 1990's, the vast majority of work generated within the sociology of punishment owed much to Foucauldian inspirations and, by the beginning of the 1990s, Foucault's work could be seen as the core of research in this area.

As early as 1991, Garland began to criticize the Foucauldian perspective, observing, for example, that Foucault invites us to:

...approach the study of penal institutions on the assumption that everything that occurs there is fundamentally oriented to the enhancement of control and the maximization of regulative power. Everything from the practice of leniency to the creation of a recidivist delinquent class is to be seen as functional for control. The possibility of non-utilitarian procedures, irrational commitments of dysfunctional elements is thus precluded in advance. If such phenomena do seem to occur they simply force us to look elsewhere for their function—to keep searching until we uncover their hidden utility for power.[13]

For Garland, to think of punishment strictly within an ends-means framework is "inappropriate." A sociology of punishment is not reducible to a sociology of control and domination (as Foucault would have it).[14] Moreover, Garland argues, punishment cannot be understood exclusively in terms of any single contributory aspect. Further cautioning against reductionism in analyses of punishment, he warns, "[I]f one wishes to understand and evaluate the prison as an institution—and the same arguments apply to the fine, probation, the death penalty, and the rest—it does little good to do so on a single plane or in relation to a single value." The same may hold true for "prison rape."

In *The Culture of Control* (2001), Garland develops a critical understanding of the practices and discourses of crime control—what he calls "the field of crime control and criminal justice"—that have come to characterize the United States and Great Britain in the late modern era. In contrast to his earlier work in *Punishment in Modern Society* (1990), which focused exclusively on penality—that is, the practices, laws, discourses, and representations that constitute the official penal system—in *The Culture of Control* Garland broadens his scope, attending to a wider field, encompassing the practices of both state and non-state actors and preventative forms of crime control as well as those perceived to be explicitly penal. As he subsequently explained, "the concept of a broad social field—as opposed to a narrower complex of state institutions—was adopted in the *Culture of Control* because the aim of the research was to address the ways in which crime now figures in the thought and action of lay people as well as legal actors, and to investigate how and why this came to be true" (Garland 2001:161). Accordingly, he explained, "I widened my analytical focus to encompass not just the state's penal responses to crime but the whole field of formal and informal practices of crime prevention, crime avoidance and control, together with forms of thought and feeling that organize and motivate these practices."

Garland places cultural phenomena center stage in his analysis of recent transformations in the field of crime control and criminal justice, a move that is central to the current research. For Garland, contemporary patterns of crime control in the U.S. and Great Britain include the emergence and subsequent decline of the modernist style of thinking about and acting upon crime, the shift from a preoccupation with law enforcement to a growing concern with security management, and the beginnings of a shift from a system of crime control monopolized by the state to a system involving state and non-state partnerships. These and other historic transformations are "adaptive responses to the cultural and criminological conditions of late modernity" (Garland 2001:161).

Empirically and theoretically, *The Culture of Control* is grand in scope, offering an historical account of the emergence of the contemporary field of crime control in the U.S. and the U.K., a sociological description of the contemporary field, and an analysis of its social functions and significance. Garland accomplishes these ends by focusing on central discourses, strategies, and policies of crime control in a way that reveals structural patterns at the level of the field, not at the level of a particular institution or agency.

Garland's analysis has been widely applauded for its "clear, cogent, and critical account of crime control and criminal justice in late modern societies" (Lyon 2003) as well as for its theoretical contributions to the field (Beckett 2001). At the same time, it has also been criticized for certain perceived shortcomings. One criticism noted by a number of scholars is especially important in this context.[15] Specifically, Garland's analysis focuses exclusively on new policies and practices that succeeded in establishing themselves in the newly transformed field and traces them to the cultural forces that led to their adoption. As Garland (2004) later acknowledged, this approach yielded a portrait of a multi-dimensional subject rendered in what amounts to two-dimensional terms.[16] Garland's analysis fails to account for the likelihood that cultural forces that *did not* succeed in finding expression in the current conjuncture were neither destroyed nor rendered impotent in the fray. Indeed, such deposed or displaced forces may continue to be operative—playing an ongoing role in the constitution of the field as they compete, resist, and otherwise press for change. Garland's analytic oversight led him to underemphasize the potential importance of complex and ongoing ideological dynamics within the present era, especially as they play out across various discursive fields.

Focusing on an extremely understudied aspect of punishment, this research builds on Garland's analytic model, developing a genealogy of "prison rape" that accounts not only for its current configuration in the legal arena and the elite and popular press, along with the cultural forces associated with these representations, but also for alternative constructions and cultural forces that failed to find expression in the current conjuncture. To do so, this analysis draws on work in the area of constitutive legal scholarship and in the area of cultural sociology. Thus, it together three formerly unrelated theoretical perspectives in order to theorize the current field of thought about sexual violence and state punishment evidenced in the two arenas of discourse described above.

Within a constitutive framework, law is regarded as a factor that helps to organize and interpret phenomena, including social relations; at the same time, social relations shape, give force to, and help determine the content of law. Moreover, the social and legal domains are conceived as both mutually embedded and on the whole reciprocally constitutive.[17] From this perspective, law is often seen to function as an instrument of hegemony, playing a part in the constitution of a social terrain circumscribed by tacit ideological interests.

However, as a more nuanced understanding of constitutive theory suggests, hegemony is neither static nor is it ever complete. Once in place, it does not remain so indefinitely nor does it preclude the existence of conflicting ideologies. Indeed, although law always contributes to and reflects ideology, its relationship to hegemony is necessarily contingent. Thus, the extent to which the cultural forces and attendant ideologies that support a given configuration represent a taken-for-granted, settled, dominant, or prevailing worldview becomes an empirical question – one that will be addressed in the current research. As any number of scholars have shown – and as is evidenced in earlier work of my own – the worldviews expressed in law and circulated in culture are not necessarily cut from the same cloth.[18]

Expanding on Garland's analytical model offers an opportunity to understand contemporaneous constructions of prison rape in the context of the various available constructions of the phenomenon circulating in culture over the time period of interest. Further, taking advantage of the insights provided by both constitutive legal scholars and by cultural sociologists, this research moves beyond describing of how prison rape is constructed at specific locations to understand the relationship among various constructions and thus to theorize the complex field of though about state punishment and sexual violence and to consider its implications for larger issues of legitimacy, the rule of law, and the interpenetration of law and society.

To accomplish these goals, this research draws on recent work in cultural sociology that complicates traditional understandings of culture and theorizes the circumstances under which culture may play a causal role in determining action. Over the course of the last three decades, the notion of culture as a "seamless web" (Swidler 1997) of shared values that remain "unitary and internally coherent across groups and situations" has given way to more complex and empirically useful conceptualizations. No longer a unified system that infuses beliefs, molds intentions, and pushes action in consistent directions (Swidler 1986), culture has come to be understood as fragmented and inconsistent, amounting to "disparate bits of information and...schematic structures that organize that information" (DiMaggio 1997: 263) or "complex rule-like structures that constitute resources which can be put to strategic use (DiMaggio 1997: 263). Many have come to understand culture as a "repertoire" (Hannerz, 1969) or "toolkit" (Swidler, 1986) comprised of elements or "cultural models"[19] social actors use to construct strategies of action. Any given social context offers an array of potentially overlapping, contradictory, contested, loosely integrated, incompatible (Sewell 1999), mutually constitutive, and/or entirely disconnected models from which to choose (Swidler 1986; Quinn and Holland 1987; Holloway, et al. 1997; Fuller et al. 1996; Harding 2006). Reflecting varying "ideas about how the world works, what appropriate goals are, and how to go about accomplishing things" (Harding 2006), cultural models are acquired through direct experience, social interaction and, at a broader level, through exposure to institutions such as the media, schooling, politics, and religion (Harding 2006). Accordingly, cultural repertoires vary across individual actors and cultural groups based on the available cultural models they contain.

Quinn and Holland (1987:4) define "cultural models" as "[p]resupposed, taken-for-granted models of the world that are widely shared (although not to the exclusion of other, alternative models) by members of a society and that play an enormous role in their understanding of that world and their behavior in it." A number of different objects have been identified as "cultural models" that may contribute to an individual or group's cultural toolkit. Swidler (1986), for example, locates "ideologies" and "traditions" under this rubric and

Harding (2006) places "frames" and "scripts" in the same category. Frames and scripts represent primary organizing and analytic category in this analysis. Harding (2006:9) defines "frames" as "ways of understanding the world and how it works...[that] encode expectations about consequences of behavior, and how various parts of the social world relate or do not relate to one another" (Harding 2006:7). Benford and Snow (2000) provide a similar definition, emphasizing the role of frames in identifying problems, assigning blame, and providing solutions (Harding 2006).

Goffman's *Frame Analysis* (1974) has been widely cited as the key origin for both the term and the concept that frames represent ways of interpreting the world. Borrowing from Goffman, Snow, et al. (1986) use the term to denote "'schemata of interpretation' that enable individuals 'to locate, perceive, identify, and label' occurrences within their life space and the world at large. By rendering events or occurrences meaningful, frames function to organize experience and guide action, whether individual or collective" (464). Along this same line, Harding (2006) defines frames as "ways of understanding the world and how it works...[that] encode expectations about consequences of behavior, and how various parts of the social world relate or do not relate to one another" (7).

Benford and Snow (2000) emphasize the role of frames in identifying problems and assigning blame. These scholars have shown how social movements rely on frame alignment to develop a shared understanding of issues, often reworking that understanding to become more inclusive and more or less focused on action (Schmeirbach 2004). To the extent that frames can be aligned in this fashion, the movement is more or less successful (Snow, Rochford, Worden, and Benford 1986). Further, as Schmeierbach (2004) points out, the work of Gamson (1989) and Gamson and Modigliani (1987) documents the master frames that are employed during particular time periods, shaping the shared understanding of an issue for policymakers and for the public as well. Implicit in all this work is the notion that there are multiple available ways that issues may be framed and that through selection of a particular frame, we select one understanding over others (Schmeirbach 2004).

Closely akin to what Swidler (2006) terms "strategies of action," "scripts provide cultural templates for the sequencing of behaviors or actions over time." "They show how to solve problems or achieve goals" (Harding, 2006:9). While scripts may be related to frames, the content of frames and scripts (like the frames themselves) are not always logically coherent (Harding, 2007). As Harding asserts:

> There need not be consistency across various scripts or frames, as individuals are often able to live with many contradictions and inconsistencies. Therefore, one should not think of frames and scripts as necessarily hierarchically nested. Instead, individuals or groups may possess or employ multiple contradictory frames and scripts. People of a common culture do not share a coherent, monolithic culture, but rather a set of available frames and scripts objective structural conditions, and knowledge of what others do and think. The ability of culture to serve as a predictor of action is predicated on variation in these available cultural models across individuals and groups (Harding 2006:346).

DATA

This research commenced with the collection of two types of archival data. Together, the resulting data sets comprise a comprehensive, empirical record of discourse about prison rape generated in the appellate courts and in elite and popular newspapers prior to January 1, 2007. In the chapters to follow, the analysis and comparison of these two original data sets render visible the myriad constitutive features of prison rape in these arenas and facilitate mapping of the complex relationships among them within and across time and social locations.

Initially, data collection efforts focused on developing a comprehensive record of discourse about prison rape generated in the elite and popular U.S. print news media. Extensive preliminary research revealed that the relatively long-standing albeit somewhat variable attention paid to prison rape matters in the printed news media has resulted in the accumulation of a rich and extensive archive of potential data for analysis. Beyond the sheer volume of published material available, the broad time span over which it was published and its textual nature render such data highly desirable for historical interpretive analysis, as well as for comparison with the data set representing legal discourse about prison rape. Although no media has been entirely reticent on the subject of prison rape, in the context of this research, the majority of other formats offered disappointingly less potential for data collection.

The analysis of news media texts presented in Chapter 2 and Chapter 3 focuses on 349 news stories, editorials, and other textual materials published in elite and popular U.S. newspapers between 1969 and 2006. To identify the data set, an initial Boolean search of "U.S Newspapers" ("All Regions") and "Newswires and Press Releases"[20] was executed using the LexisNexis Academic database and employing a number of related search terms including "priso! rape," "priso! sexual assault," and "priso! sexual abuse."[21] The parameters of the search were further defined using the "Specify Date" function to limit retrieval to opinions published prior to January 1, 2007. This search resulted in retrieval of 382 articles, the earliest of which was published in December 1979. Because LexisNexis provides limited access to news articles published prior to 1980, an additional step was taken to ensure comprehensive collection of data for this analysis. Employing the original search terms and temporal parameters, a search was executed of NewspaperArchive.com, an online archival database containing over 75 million newspaper pages dating from 1759 to present.[22] This search retrieved over 2000 articles, the vast majority of which did not, in fact, contain the specific search terms employed.[23] Once the erroneously retrieved articles were identified and discarded, this search netted 78 relevant news articles, the earliest published in March 1969. Combined, the LexisNexis and NewspaperArchive searches generated 460 articles, 102 of which were discarded when, upon examination, they were found to duplicate other articles collected. The remaining 358 articles became the pool from which a data set would be identified.

To qualify for analysis, articles in the preliminary pool had to meet only one additional criterion. That is, they had to contain at least one substantive reference to rape, sexual assault, or sexual abuse of an individual, individuals, or class of individuals detained or incarcerated in prison, jail, or other carceral facility in the United States.[24] Based on preliminary reading, nine articles that did not meet this criterion were discarded, along with an additional 102 articles that duplicated other articles in the pool. The remaining 349 articles comprise the data set for this analysis. With publication dates ranging from March 4, 1969 to December 14, 2006, these data were organized and arranged in order to form a comprehensive empirical record of all relevant print news media texts published in the sampled newspapers prior to January 1, 2007.

The analysis of legal discourse presented in Chapter 4 and Chapter 5 focuses on a data set consisting of 171 state and federal appellate court opinions published between 1969 and 2006. Over the past several decades, researchers have successfully enlisted appellate opinions and other legal artifacts as data for analysis, most frequently in studies of legal narrative, judicial language, legal meaning making, and judicial outcomes (Connolly 1998; Philips and Grattet 2000; Albiston 2003; Pinello 2003; Richman 2004; Smyth 2006). As data, appellate opinions offer some practical and methodological advantages for historical-interpretive and comparative legal research. The fact that nearly all state and federal-level appellate opinions are published, electronically formatted, and easily accessed using searchable databases serves to promote empirically comprehensive data collection, thereby increasing external validity and importantly, allowing for the introduction of an historical perspective. Further, published appellate opinions tend to follow a fairly standard format – first presenting a brief statement of the issue(s) on appeal and a procedural history of these matter(s), followed by a detailed factual background of the case presented in narrative form, an elaboration of relevant case law, and finally presentation of the court's opinion and, in some cases, one or more dissenting opinions. This "formulaic" organization facilitates coding of data and comparison of cases along an array of analytic dimensions (Philips and Grattet, 2000).

To generate a pool of appellate opinions from which a data set for this analysis would be identified, a Boolean search was executed of all state and federal case law using LEXIS legal software employing the same search terms as were used to generate the pool of news articles.[25] The parameters of the search were further defined using the "Specify Date" function to limit retrieval to opinions published before January 1, 2007. So delimited, the LEXIS search resulted in retrieval of 645 civil and criminal appellate opinions with publication dates ranging from January 1947 through October 2006. These became the pool from which the data set would be extracted. To be included in this analysis, opinions in the preliminary pool had to meet two additional criteria. First, each case had to contain one or more references to rape, sexual assault, or sexual abuse of an individual, individuals, or class of individuals detained or incarcerated in a prison, jail, or other carceral facility in the United States. Second, the reference(s) to rape, sexual assault, or sexual abuse found in the appellate opinion had to pertain to the specific case under appeal. Preliminary reading allowed me to eliminate 474 of the original 645 opinions retrieved based on their failure to meet both of these criteria. The remaining 171 opinions qualified for analysis. Beginning with *People v. Wayne Robert Richards* (February 18, 1969) and ending with *James Doe v. Gene A. Scroggy* (October 23, 2006), these data were organized and arranged in order to form a comprehensive empirical record of all state and federal appellate-level opinions containing prison rape discourse published prior to January 1, 2007.

METHOD OF ANALYSIS

The overarching goal of this research was to identify and compare cultural repertoires for understanding and responding to "prison rape" as they evolved over time in the legal arena and in the elite and popular print news media. To accomplish this end, a frame analysis of legal and media discourse was undertaken. Drawing on Benford and Snow's (2000) notion of the role of frames in identifying problems and assigning blame, attention was focused on identifying frames employed for those specific purposes. Close reading of the data allowed me to identify the overarching frames employed to diagnose the problem of prison rape, to assign blame for the problem, and to offer solutions for it. Although multiple frames of varying levels of specificity *can* apply in any given context (Harding 2006), for this analysis the focus was on the *dominant* frames employed in diagnosing the problem of prison rape over time, and assigning blame for the problem. Thus, once the various frames were identified and their parameters specified, each opinion and article was coded for the single frame that dominated that particular aspect of the discussion of prison rape. Each data set was read in chronological order and coded "1" for the dominant frame deployed and "0" on the remaining frames. The information gleaned from this analysis was entered into the SPSS database created earlier, a move which enabled me to track the dominant frames deployed in legal and news media representations prison rape over time.

Once these frames were identified, the data were coded in accordance with the dominant frames employed to discuss prison rape on those specific dimensions in each news article and appellate opinion. This process yielded quantitative data which allowed me to track the various ways in which prison rape was framed in discourse produced in each of the two social locations over time. Thereafter, a systematic content analysis was undertaken aimed at identifying and coding cultural "scripts" associated with various ways of framing prison rape discourse within each social location over time. A database containing the information gleaned from these first two parts of the analysis was constructed in Statistical Program for the Social Sciences (SPSS), a move that allowed me to conduct simple statistical tabulations along key analytic dimensions, as well as to generate graphic representations of frequencies and fluctuations in the deployment of these cultural objects over time. Finally, an interpretive content analysis of the discourse generated in each social location was undertaken to create a rich and nuanced empirical portrait of prison rape as it was constituted within the frames and scripts identified earlier.

Within the initial stages of the analysis, patterns emerged in the data which suggested the delineation of two distinct time periods within the forty-three-year time frame of this research. While admittedly fuzzy around the edges, each of the two periods can be distinguished from the other based on discernable variations in the quantity of discourse produced annually, as well as shifts in content from one time period to the next. In the chapters to follow, these time periods – specifically an historical period (1969-1991) and a contemporary period (1992-2006) – provide a temporal framework for the analysis and comparison of data within and across and social locations and represent a central organizing feature of this investigation.

Based on the knowledge that discourse is not generated in a vacuum, throughout this analysis the author remained attentive to the broader historico-cultural context within which the iteration of legal and journalistic discourse occurred. While remaining focused primarily on the specific data and time frame described above, interpretation of the narratives was fleshed out and contextualized by referencing discourses produced previously, contemporaneously, or nearly contemporaneously in other media formats and social locations. In particular, "spot checks" were employed of popular news and entertainment magazine articles about prisons, prisoners, and prison rape, as well as published studies on prisons, prison sex, and sexual violence conducted and narrated by social science researchers. Articles that contributed to this effort were identified using the *Reader's Guide to Periodical Literature* as well as Gaes and Goldberg's (2004) inventory of social science research on prison rape.

---

[1] *Reports of the Prison Discipline Society of Boston.* 1972. (Publication No. 155: Reprint Series in Criminology, Law Enforcement, and Social Problems). Patterson Smith: Montclair, New Jersey.

[2] http://www.jewishworldreview.com/cols/chavez070203.asp, last visited 01/02/08.

[3] http://findarticles.com/p/articles/mi_m0EIN/is_2003_July_22/ai_105653450, last visited 12/31/2007.

[4] http://www.foxnews.com/story/0,2933,97392,00.html, last visited 01/01/08.

[5] Prison Rape Elimination Act of 2003, 42 U.S.C. § 15601-15609.

[6] Fleischer, Mark (2008). *The Myth of Prison Rape: Sexual Culture in American Prisons.* Rowman & Littlefield Publishers, Inc.:Lanham, MD.

[7] Justice Clarence Thomas is among the few holding the belief that, although regrettable, prison rape amounts to a potentially unavoidable condition of confinement and as such cannot be understood as "punishment." In *Farmer v. Brennan* (1994), Thomas opined, "Prisons are necessarily dangerous places; they house society's most antisocial and violent people in close proximity with one another. Regrettably, some level of brutality and sexual aggression among prisoners is inevitable no matter what the guards do...unless all prisoners are locked in their cells 24 hours a day and sedated....I adhere to my belief, expressed in *Hudson and Helling* v. *McKinney*, that judges or juries—but not jailers—impose punishment. Punishment, from the time of the Founding through the present day, has always meant a "fine, penalty, or confinement inflicted upon a person by the authority of the law and the judgment and sentence of a court, for some crime or offense committed by him. Conditions of confinement are not punishment in any recognized sense of the term.

[8] Garland, D. (1991). "Sociological Perspectives on Punishment." *Crime and Justice*, Vol. 14, 115-165.

[9] Ibid., p. 120.

[10] Ibid.

[11] Foucault, Michel. (1976) 1995. *Discipline and Punish: The Birth of the Prison.* New York, NY: Vintage Books.

[12] Garland David. (1990). "Frameworks of Inquiry in the Sociology of Punishment." *The British Journal of Sociology*, Vol. 41, No. 1 (Mar. 1990), 1-15.

[13] Ibid., p. 6.

[14] Ibid. p. 7.

[15] See, for example, Savelsberg, J.J. (2002). "Cultures of Control in Contemporary Societies." *Law and Social Inquiry*, Vol. 27, No. 3, 685-710; Young, J. (2003). "Searching for a New Criminology of Everyday Life: A Review of the Culture of Control." *British Journal of Criminology*, Vol. 43, No. 1, 228-43.

[16] Garland, David. (2004). "Beyond the Culture of Control." *Critical Review of International Social and Political Philosophy*, Vol. 7, No. 2, 160-89.

[17] Mertz, Elizabeth. (1988). "The Uses of History: Language, Ideology and the Law in the United States and South Africa." *Law and Society Review*, 34, 567-606; Hunt, Alan. (1990). "Rights and Social Movements: Counter-Hegemonic Strategies." *Journal of Law and Society*, 17, 309-328; Conley, John M., & William M. O'Barr. (1990). *Rules Versus Relationships: The Ethnography of Legal Discourse*. Chicago: University of Chicago Press; Conley, John M., & William M. O'Barr (1998). *Just Words: Law, Language, and Power*. Chicago: University of Chicago Press; Sarat, Austin & Thomas R. Kearns (Eds.). (1993). *Law in Everyday Life*. Ann Arbor: University of Michigan Press; Coutin, Susan Bibler. (1994). "Enacting law through social practice: sanctuary as a form of resistance," in S. Hirsch & M. Lazarus-Black, eds. *Contested States: Law, Hegemony and Resistance*; Hirsch, Susan F. & Mindie Lazarus-Black. (1994). "Introduction/Performance and Paradox: Exploring Law's Role in Hegemony and Resistance," in M. Lazarus-Black & S. F. Hirsch, (eds.), *Contested States: Law, Hegemony and Resistance*. New York: Routledge.

[18] Smyth, Michael. "Queers and Provocateurs: Hegemony, Ideology and the 'Homosexual Advance' Defense." *Law and Society Review*, 40, 903-930.

[19] Quinn and Holland (1987:4), and later Harding (2006:7) rely on the following definition of "cultural models": *Presupposed, taken-for-granted models of the world that are widely shared (although not to the exclusion of other, alternative models) by the members of a society and that play an enormous role in their understanding of that world and their behavior in it.* Swidler (1986) locates "ideologies" under the "cultural models" rubric. Harding adds "frames" and "scripts" to the list of cultural objects that constitute the cultural toolkit.

[20] Appendix B provides a complete inventory of the news sources searched using the parameters described.

[21] The inventory of search terms employed included: "priso! rape"; "rape priso!"; "inmate rape"; "rape inmate"; "priso! sexual assault"; "sexual assault priso!"; "sexual assault inmate"; "inmate sexual assault"; "sexual abuse priso!"; "priso! sexual abuse"; "sexual abuse inmate"; and "inmate sexual abuse."

[22] NewspaperArchive.com (http://www.newspaperarchive.com/) is billed as the largest online historical newspaper database, containing over 75 million newspaper pages dating from 1759 to the present.

[23] This was true in spite of the fact that searches of the NewspaperArchive database were conducted using the "exact phrase" function. A majority of the articles retrieved contained phrases such as "X was sent to prison on the rape charge," which rendered them irrelevant for the purposes of this analysis.

[24] A "substantive" reference might better be described as "code-able." References to prison rape that were not considered appropriate for analysis included, for example, a reference to a musical group called "Prison Rape," a song titled "Prison Rape," and the use of "prison rape" as a simile for an undesirable event.

[25] The inventory of search terms employed included: "priso! rape"; "rape priso!"; "inmate rape"; "rape inmate"; "priso! sexual assault"; "sexual assault priso!"; "sexual assault inmate"; "inmate sexual assault"; "sexual abuse priso!"; "priso! sexual abuse"; "sexual abuse inmate"; and "inmate sexual abuse."

CHAPTER TWO

Prison Rape in the Popular Press, 1969-1991: The Historic Period

INTRODUCTION

Prison rape emerged as an object of interest in U.S. newspapers in 1969, an historical moment when criminal justice and criminals were changing materially, procedurally, and discursively. Significant increases in the national crime rate, which had begun to climb sharply after the 1950s, served to position crime, punishment, and criminals in the foreground of public discourse. While crime and punishment had to some extent always been part of the public consciousness, it was not until the 1960s that these matters became a pressing topic of a public discussion. (Sloop 1996). Moreover, by the latter half of that decade, the crime problem was intense enough in the public mind to become one of the central factors upon which voters based their political decisions (Friedman 1993).

Coincident with the increased volume of public discourse about crime and punishment, changes were occurring in the theory and practice of criminal justice. While the perspective Dilulio (1991) labeled as "old penology" had dominated penological thought from the nineteenth century until it began to decline in popularity in the 1940s, the "new penology" which followed refocused the way policymakers understood and discussed criminal behavior and the treatment of prisoners. This new penal philosophy "turned the two main precepts of the old penology on their heads....Whereas the old penology focused sympathetically on prison administrators and others who carried on the business of criminal justice, the new penology focused its sympathies on prisoners; and whereas the old penology maintained that prisons must be governed strictly – from the top down – by duly appointed officials, the new penology maintained that prisons must be governed by prisoners themselves" (DiIulio 1991:72). The move to the new penology grew stronger throughout the 1950s and 1960s, such that, by 1969, its basic tenets – that "prisoners must be allowed, to some limited degree, to maintain their own systems of rules and justice, to act as and be treated as competent human beings" (DiIulio 1991:72) – came to regarded by penologists as assumed knowledge. By the time the influence of the new penology reached its peak in 1980, John Irwin, author of *Prisons in Turmoil* (1980), depicted prison officials as "little better than ill educated racists" (DiIulio 1991:72), while prisoners were understood as "humans just like us...[who] will act honorably, given a real choice" (124-26).

As public interest in crime and criminal justice matters grew throughout the 1950s and 1960s, violence was on the increase at carceral facilities around the country. The rash of mid-century prison riots and escapes was served to the public in large portions by the print news media. Articles like "Behind Those Prison Riots" in the widely circulated *Reader's Digest*,[1] "Prisoners on Strike – The Meaning,"[2] and "Why Convicts Riot" in *U.S. News and World Report*[3] fed the public's concern about these matters as they attempted to explain why prisoners, the majority of whom were understood to be fundamentally rational and redeemable individuals, continued to perpetrate violence and generally wreak havoc within carceral walls. Overwhelmingly, the mid-century press represented the growing epidemic of violence as a signifier of prisons' general malignancy, their inhumane treatment of prisoners, and the utter lack of opportunities for offenders to rehabilitate themselves in carceral settings. Thus, rather than representing prison violence as the irrational conduct of dangerous and incorrigible convicts, these incidents were most often understood as manifestations of a failing system that was mistreating the prisoners in its charge. As the authors of "A Riot is an Unnecessary Evil," a 1952 *Life* magazine article pointed out, "it takes a long period of abuses to set the stage for a full fledged riot."[4]

Although prisoners remained fundamentally redeemable in the minds of both penologists and the press throughout the middle decades of the last century, by the end of the 1960s even the most ardent supporters of the rehabilitative model had come to admit that not all prisoners were viable candidates for rehabilitation. Indeed, by this time a new type of prisoner emerged in the media to stand alongside the more familiar, redeemable prisoner. These individuals – fundamentally immoral, often irrational, and innately violent or violence-prone career criminals – were represented as "impervious to such normal emotions as compassion, pity, and guilt" (Sloop 1996:75). Utterly beyond redemption, these hopeless incorrigibles, it was understood, were destined to endure a future characterized by continuous or successive episodes of incarceration and punishment, not rehabilitation.

In the cultural milieu described above, prison rape emerged as a subject of interest and concern in the U.S. print news media in 1969. Over the course of the 23-years following its initial appearance in the press, more than 50 articles pertaining to prison rape appeared in U.S. newspapers, an average of about two articles published annually between 1969 and 1991. Clearly, this constituted a notable increase in the volume of discourse about prison rape relative to preceding years when the press had remained entirely silent on the subject. At the same time, it should be noted that the 51 articles published during the "historical period" amounted to less than 15% of the total articles on the topic published across the 38-year time period of interest in this analysis. Indeed, more than 85% of the articles that comprise this data set were published during the 15-year-long "contemporary period" between 1992 and 2006.

Like the dramatic increase that differentiated the volume of discourse circulated in the contemporary era press from the historic period, the distribution of articles published *within* the historic period offers some interesting insights as well. Ranging from a high of 10 articles published in 1979 and in 1982, to a low of zero, or no articles at all published in the seven years including 1971, 1973, 1984, 1986-87, 1989-1990, it is apparent that news media discourse about prison rape was distributed unevenly across the historic period. Further, the pattern of distribution indicates that the bulk of attention paid to prison rape in the historical-era press occurred during the first half of the period. Of the total articles pertaining to prison rape published between 1969 and 1991, nearly 80% appeared prior to 1981, the midpoint of the historic period. Thereafter, the annual number of articles on the subject dropped sharply, such that during the final nine years of the historical period, only three prison rape-related articles were published in U.S.

newspapers. Thus, while the media's initial "discovery" of prison rape as a topic of interest was followed by a relatively brief flurry of attention in the elite and popular press, by 1983 the news media had once again fallen virtually silent on the subject.

In sharp contrast to the rather dramatic variations noted in the distribution of media discourse about prison rape prior to 1992, the way in which the press framed the subject remained relatively consistent across the entire 23-year historical period. As the analysis to follow will illustrate, historical-era news articles framed prison rape first and foremost as a symptom of institutional failure – specifically the failure of the nation's prison systems. Within this dominant frame, however, the press deployed a number of scripts depicting the relationship between prison rape and correctional failures in various ways, some related, some unrelated – and attributing blame for the problem to a surprisingly broad array of culprits.

DIAGNOSING THE PROBLEM

Institutional Failure

The subject of prison rape debuted in the American print news media framed in a discourse about institutional failure – specifically the failure of a U.S. prison system widely understood to be out of control and acutely in need of reform. Among the articles published during the historical period, the vast majority framed prison rape in these terms. In this context, the press deployed a variety of related scripts representing prison rape on one hand as a byproduct of corrections' general malignancy and on the other as a symptom of prisons' failure to perform on a number of specific, critical dimensions, including the control of prisoners and maintenance of order, the rehabilitation of lawbreakers, and protection of the community outside prison walls.

Articles that represented prison rape as a symptom of the general failure of corrections depicted American carceral facilities as "monster-producing factories,"[5] "human warehouses,"[6] "cesspools of degradation"[7] where "abominable conditions"[8] like the threat of sexual assault prevailed on a daily basis. *The Ruston Daily Leader* and *The Pharos-Tribune and Press* called prison rape "a massive evil" that rendered conditions in U.S. prisons shocking to even the most "experienced police officers and detectives, who were quite used to seeing humanity at its worst." [9] An article in a 1982 series of *Washington Post* exposés on epidemic rape in American jails indicated that U.S. facilities were so deplorable that judges had become reluctant to sentence even convicted felons to "do time" because rape would be among the conditions they would likely experience while incarcerated.[10] Another article in the same series attributed the following statement to District Court Judge Vincent Femia: "If we knew we could send someone to jail without him being sexually assaulted, there'd be a lot more people going to jail. The rapes work to the disadvantage of a judge who wants to send someone to jail...to teach him a lesson." A 1975 article published in the Troy, New York *Times Record* provided alarming first person testimony from a convict who had fled from prison to escape the threat of "homosexual rape." The inmate declared that he would "rather die than go back" to the deplorable conditions he faced as an inmate at the Florida institution where he had been incarcerated.[11] And, finally, that same year, *The New York Times* reported that the threat of "homosexual rape" had become so fearsome that a California appellate court declared that, in some instances, escape from prison might be justified to avoid such attacks.[12]

In the context of this discourse, epidemic rape in U.S. prisons was represented as indicative of a dysfunctional and failing institution – malignant to its core and potentially unsalvageable. As "Sexual Abuse of Inmates Bared in Senate," a 1969 article in the *Chicago Daily Defender*, alleged, "[A] major reform of the entire prison system would be required in order to stamp out this situation permanently."[13] The script characterizing prison rape as a signifier of prisons' general failure characterized about one third of the articles that appeared during the historical period, although it was most commonly deployed during the earlier years of this period. Indeed, nearly all of the articles that drew on this script were published prior to 1981, the midpoint of this 23-year period.

Failure to Control Prisoners

A number of news articles published during this period deployed scripts representing prison rape not so much as a symptom of prisons' general failure but rather their failure to perform on specific dimensions essential to their mandated purpose. For example, among the articles published prior to 1992, about half represented prison rape as an indication that prisons were either unwilling or incapable of controlling the prisoners placed in their charge. Indeed, the appeal of the "new penology" appears to have been largely lost on the press. Articles published during this period suggest little enthusiasm about the idea of inmates controlling the conditions of their own confinement. In 1969, when prison rape began to be discussed in U.S. newspapers, journalists had already begun to cast a skeptical eye on this "new" correctional philosophy and the conditions – among them, prison rape – they perceived as concomitant with it. *"De Profundis,"* for example, a 1969 article published in the Danville, Virginia *Register*, suggested that prison rape is a byproduct of prisons "controlled by inmates – not prison personnel" and identified those "kingpins" running prisons as "the strongest and most vicious of all." [14] "Control of inmates is impossible," *"De Profundis"* declared. "So bad are conditions in many places," *U.S. News and World Report* asserted, "the inmates, not the guards, set their own rules and punishment."[15] Likewise, a 1970 article in *The Derrick*, published in the tri-city area of Oil City-Franklin-Clarion, Pennsylvania, described a local penal institution where sexual assaults were allegedly commonplace as a "great big human warehouse where strong convicts control the entire prison."[16] As Sheriff Thomas Purvis remarked in the 1977 *U.S. News and World Report* article cited above, "The only thing we control is their movement. If one inmate decides to rape another…the only rule is survival of the fittest."[17]

Like the articles that deployed a "general failure" script, the vast majority of these articles, appeared prior to the midpoint of the historical period.

Failure to Rehabilitate Prisoners

If prisons were incapable of controlling prisoners, they certainly couldn't rehabilitate them. Throughout this period, a number of news articles suggested that prison rape amounted to an indication that U.S. jails and prisons were failing at the job of rehabilitating prisoners – a task that at least the press still perceived to be one of corrections' most important duties. Whether explicitly or implicitly, articles deploying this script conflated prison rape and failure or inability to rehabilitate such that the former could be understood as both a cause and an effect of prisons' failure along one of the most critical dimensions of correctional performance.

Fueling the claim that U.S. penal institutions were "monster-producing factories,"[18] and "schools for crime"[19] where "correction is out of the question"[20] and "rehabilitation programs are nonexistent,"[21] "Sexual Abuse of Inmates Bared in Senate," the first article on prison rape to appear in a U.S. newspaper, declared that the "[a]bominable conditions" in U.S. prisons "must be overcome so institutions can rehabilitate youthful offenders rather than converting them into hardened criminals." "We're not rehabilitating people" District Court Judge Joseph Casula told *The Washington Post*. Ironically, many of the attributes that placed a prisoner at high risk for sexual victimization and unable to defend himself against it were the same qualities that were understood to render him ripe for rehabilitation. Indeed, "the ideal target of prison rape is easily recognized by prisoners and prison officials alike: the young, the slightly built, the 'new fish'."[22] By virtue of his youth, his inexperience, his attachment to a life and family outside prison walls, and his non-violent nature, this prisoner was regarded as a prime candidate for rehabilitation, a virtual magnate for sexual violence, and utterly without the physical prowess to defend against it.

In "Justice May Not Be Served," defense attorney James E. Kenkel stated "'[T]he rapes are certainly counterproductive to any attempt to rehabilitate….We know that victims become aggressors just as abused children become abusers. In another time and place, jail rape victims are likely to abuse others.'"[23] Along these same lines, *The Washington Post* noted that to avoid prison rape, many prisoners are obliged to behave "much more violently in jail than they normally do. After months of such behavior…they became capable of committing crimes that were far more serious than the ones that sent them to jail."[24]

As was the case with the scripts discussed in the preceding section, the distribution of articles that construed prison rape as indicative of prisons' failure to rehabilitate prisoners was uneven over this 23-year period. Among the articles that deployed this script, the majority were published during the first half of the time period. By the end of the 1980s, the issue of prisoner rehabilitation had disappeared entirely from discussions pertaining to prison rape and it failed to reemerge again.

Failure to Protect the Community

If prison rape was a indicator that U.S. prisons amounted to "monster producing factories" that were failing at both the control and rehabilitation of prisoners in their charge, they were also understood to be failing to protect the safety of the community outside prison walls. We are "sending monsters out into the community," said one Common Pleas Court judge.[25]   Similarly, then Philadelphia District Attorney Arlen Specter remarked in 1969, "Can any one of us understand what degradation and hatred a young man must feel when he is released into the community after being homosexually raped?   The harm spread through our community by such embittered men is incalculable."[26] "American Penology Failure" declared that "the conditions of the more than 3,000 local jails in the United States, without question contributes directly to the crime problem"[27] in our communities and "Unimposed Punishment," an article in the February 8, 1977 edition of the *Xenia Daily Gazette*, identified prison rape as "not unrelated to violent street crimes" perpetrated in the community by inmates departing from U.S. penal institutions. *The Washington Post* warned, "Eventually, these people get out of jail with a lot of experience in behaving violently...Prison rape has "serious consequences for the community."[28]   *The Post* further asserted, "They create monsters in jail...When these inmates who are subjected to [prison rape] are turned loose again, they're mad and they terrorize everyone."[29]   "The real victims of [prison rape] are innocent citizens,"[30] *The Post* concluded. "Society pays a big price for allowing this situation to exist."[31]

A considerable number of articles published during this period deployed a script representing prison rape as an indicator that prisons were failing at the task of protecting the safety of the community outside prison walls.   Articles that represented prison rape in these terms were only slightly more numerous during the earlier half of this period than thereafter.   It should also be noted, however, that each of the articles that appeared after 1981 comprised a part of the *Washington Post's* exposé on prison rape.   Apart from the *Post's* series, the safety of the community was not a concern voiced in the post-1981 print-news media articles pertaining to prison rape.

Deterrence

While rape in U.S. prisons was generally framed as a symptom of correctional failures, in at least some instances it was rendered meaningful in discussions about prisons' successes – specifically their alleged ability to deter potential criminal behavior. A number of news articles published during this time period framed prison rape within a discourse about deterrence and, in that context, deployed a script representing prison rape as an effective deterrent to potential lawbreakers – juveniles in particular. Print media articles reporting on the "Scared Straight" program at Rahway prison and its progeny exemplify the use of this script. Published in 1979, this group of eight articles described a "so-called shock therapy program...where juvenile offenders are exposed to life inside [prison walls.]"[32] There, *The Boston Globe* reported:

> Twice each day, with the support of the prison officials and the community, a group of juveniles enters the prison to serve a three-hour bear-pit encounter with the hardened criminals. There the convicts describe in crude and obscene detail the realities – the homosexual rapes...that are a daily part of prison life.[33]

Similarly, *The Washington Post* described a documentary film about the program that had aired on local station WTTG-TV in the area.

> "The film telescopes into one hour a program run at Rahway state prison in New Jersey in which hardened inmates tell a group of 17 juvenile delinquents what they face in prison unless they straighten out. No details are spared. Homosexual rapes and liaisons are detailed by the inmates in the most brutal, degrading terms.[34]

The brutality of the terms in which prison rape was described was illustrated in the Annapolis, Maryland *Evening Capital,* which quoted from the film:

...someone will see you go in a cell and they'll wait on line
and when one is finished the others will come in and there will
be 15 mother------- f------ you. You'll come out crying and
your ass---- will be bleeding.[35]

In assessing the worth of the "Scared Straight" program as a crime
deterrent, *The Washington Post* concluded:

> Nothing succeeds like fear. Most of the kids who were sent
> into the Rahway program by judges went straight. The
> program has an astounding success rate. Only one of the 17
> kids in the film got into trouble in the next year. "Scared
> Straight" got huge ratings for WTTG, was reviewed in all the
> papers, and has provoked a community plagued by juvenile
> crime into focusing, at least for a moment, on a novel way to
> combat it.[36]

Exaggerations and Lies

In the vast majority of newspaper articles published during this period,
carceral rape was construed as a "massive evil" of "epidemic"
proportion in U.S. penal facilities. In contrast, a handful of articles
represented prison rape either as an outright fabrication or an
exaggerated allegation. Two 1974 articles, "He Took a 36-year Course
in Penology," and "Man Becomes Prison Expert Behind Bars," are
notable in this regard. Each of these articles profiled James Spivey, an
ex-convict who, after spending 36 years behind bars for murder, was
serving as Michigan's "legislative corrections ombudsman," a position
that cast the former prisoner in the role of prison reformer, problem
solver, and resident authority on the state's prison system. Questioned
about the incidence of prison rape, Spivey reported that "homosexual
rape [is] not as bad as people think. Young prisoners work to have
things better. They will say they're being sexually harassed to get
transferred out of an institution to a camp situation. It's used more
often than you'd think."[37] Expressing similar doubts about the veracity
of rape claims by prisoners at another facility, Arnett Gaston, director
of the in the Prince William County Jail in Virginia remarked in 1984,
"You have a statement by one person with a history of bizarre behavior
corroborated by another person with a history of bizarre

behavior...What does that prove?" Gaston continued to "buck the trend" by downplaying the seriousness of the few sexual assaults he believed actually *do* occur in U.S. jails and prisons. "These things occur because of jails' monosexual atmosphere," he said. "The exact same things happen in boarding schools."[38]

ASSIGNING BLAME

Blaming Correctional Personnel

Although the press framed prison rape as a symptom of the failure of the U.S. correctional system, for the most part the onus for prisons' failure was only rarely placed directly on the shoulders of correctional personnel. A handful of news articles, however, deployed a script attributing blame for at least part of the problem on malevolent prison guards, who laughed about sexual assaults rather than preventing them and in some instances even "encourage[d] sexual perversion."[39] As *The Ruston Daily Leader* claimed, "[G]uards on duty often showed indifference," noting an occasion, when "a young man screamed more than an hour while being gang raped in his cell, only to have the guard laugh at him when he later emerged bloody and beaten."[40] Notwithstanding the rarity with which this script was deployed in the historical-era press, the few articles that did deploy it painted a troubling picture of a U.S. prison system in which the neglect or purposeful inaction of "rogue officers" and other "bad apples" among correctional staff led to dire consequences for certain prisoners and rendered correctional officers suspect.

A trio of news articles suggested that negligence and indifference on the part of correctional officers might be more than just morally reprehensible. Journalists covering a number of court cases heard during this time period noted that guards' indifference might, in fact, amount to cause for courts to award damages to inmates who were victims of prison rape. On September 11, 1979, The Associated Press (AP) reported that a federal judge had upheld a jury's award of $130,000 to an inmate who had been "homosexually raped" at Southern Michigan Prison several years earlier. After delivering his opinion, U.S. District Judge Philip Pratt told the AP reporter, "This evidence of deliberate indifference or callous neglect combined with the evidence that officers knew of the danger of homosexual rape and inexplicably delayed reporting the incident was enough to justify the jury's verdict."[41]   Later the same year, a second AP article noted that a "juvenile victim of a homosexual rape at the Richmond City Jail" had received a $35,000 out-of-court settlement, the second such settlement...in a week" from the City of Richmond, Virginia."[42] In the earlier settlement, an inmate had received $10,000 in damages for a rape that occurred in the Richmond City Jail.[43]   Finally, in 1982, *The Washington Post* noted that the issue of officers' liability in prison rape cases had reached the highest court in the nation. "High Court Weighs Guard Liability" reported that the U.S. Supreme Court was considering whether prison rape victims seeking punitive damages from guards who put them in cells with inmates likely to harm them must show malice on the guards' part."[44]

    While some articles blamed correctional officers for prison rape, others published during this period deployed a script blaming prison rape on apathetic correctional officials who tolerated behaviors that led to sexual assault and responded to concerns about prison rape with artificially low statistics or an embarrassed or "sadistic silence."[45] "The disgrace of being sexually victimized creates a Catch-22 blueprint that prison officials, by silence or ignorance, permit to continue," said David Rothenberg in *The New York Times*. "Prison officials...continue to offer low statistics on prison rape [and] claim nothing can be done..."[46] "Punishment," an article published in *The Washington Post*, argued, "When it comes to seeing and hearing no evil, [correctional officials] make the legendary three monkeys alarmists by comparison."[47]   Along these same lines, an article in the *Los Angeles Times* blamed the problem of prison rape on corrections personnel in general, suggesting that "minimum standards for detention facilities are 'flagrantly violated' on a day-to-day basis by jail officials."[48]

    Together, the articles described above amount to a powerful condemnation of correctional personnel – one founded on allegations of pervasive indifference to prisoner safety, as well as on behaviors described as *malevolent inaction* to abate the harms suffered by prisoners.   It must be noted, however, that historical-era articles attributing blame for prison rape to correctional personnel were relatively few and far between. In fact, when correctional personnel were mentioned at all in articles published during this period, they were most often represented as inept buffoons and/or ineffectual victims of an outmoded and under-funded system than as the true villains in the story of prison rape.[49] As Richard Cohen stated in a 1982 *Washington Post* article, "[Correctional personnel] are nothing more than the fall guys for a…society that has turned in frustration over crime to simply locking up more and more people."[50]

Blaming "The System"

If prison personnel were simply "the fall guys," they were taking the fall first and foremost for a dysfunctional correctional system suffering from a number of related issues that effectively rendered correctional personnel incapable of addressing the problem of sexual assaults within carceral walls. *The Washington Post* touched on several of these in the following passage from a 1982 article titled "Terror Behind Bars":

> "Guards say they are unable to protect inmates from rapes because the poorly designed jail makes it impossible for guards to see into most cells from their watch posts. The guards say they could minimize that problem by patrolling the cells more often than once every eight hours, but that there aren't enough of them to do that. Also, they say, there would be fewer rapes and sexual assaults if inmates had individual cells. Because of overcrowding, they say, most of the cells are left unlocked to give inmates room to move about."[51]

Throughout the historical era, the ongoing disparity between optimum ratios of staff to prisoners and prisoners to intended capacity of penal facilities was one of the most frequently cited sources of blame for the problem of prison rape. Alan J. Davis, a special master for the Philadelphia Court of Common Pleas, told a UPI reporter that the alleged epidemic of prison rape in Philadelphia area jails could be attributed to "a shocking lack of guards on duty."[52] Similarly, *The Los Angeles Times* claimed, "Inmate rapes occur…because there are too few deputies to monitor activities in the various cells."[53] "Prisoners outnumber prison personnel by 180-1," the Danville, Virginia *Register* reported.[54] And, as one victim of an attempted sexual assault in a Florida prison asserted, "I was kicking and hollering and never saw a guard anywhere."[55] To address the problem, a 1970 article in a Pennsylvania newspaper noted that a Buck's County jail had "moved ahead to improve conditions" related to prison rape by "hiring more guards at higher pay."[56]   Among the articles that mentioned understaffing as a causal factor, the majority appeared prior to 1971 and all six articles appeared before the midpoint of the historical era. Interestingly, while understaffing had literally disappeared from the discourse in the print news media by 1981, overcrowded correctional facilities increasingly came to be understood as at least partly to blame for the problem of sexual assault in carceral settings. Indeed, among the articles published in the latter half of the historical period, nearly half attributed at least partial blame for the "epidemic" of prison rape to overcrowding in U.S. carceral facilities. A 1982 article in *The Washington Post*, for example, reported that both guards and inmates had cited overcrowding as a principal cause of prison rapes and sexual assaults. "Overcrowding contributes to sexual assaults because it increases tension among inmates," *The Post* noted.

In 1980, *The Los Angeles Times* reported on overcrowding at a local facility where sexual assaults were alleged to be occurring. "The maximum number of inmates the jail is supposed to house is 813...but the inmate population never dipped below 900...and fairly consistently exceeded 1000." In the same article, *Times* staff writer, Ted Vollmer, remarked on the connection between overcrowded prisons, understaffing, and prison rape. "Overcrowding spawns other problems throughout the system," Vollmer noted, "including understaffing [and] rapes of inmates."[57]   Finally, in 1982, *The Washington Post* suggested that to "relieve overcrowding" would greatly "cut down on the number of inmate rapes and other sexual assaults."[58]

Occasionally during this period, news articles noted that U.S. jails and prisons were not only inadequate in size and number, but that their antiquated condition and poor design contributed to the ongoing problem of controlling sexual assault within their walls. "*De Profundis*," in the Danville, Virginia *Register*, described "totally inadequate confinement facilities"[59] in Virginia's prisons and one Pennsylvania newspaper declared, "Prison rape is a result of warehousing prisoners in "antiquated prisons."[60]   Pointing more directly to the source of the problem, Richard Cohen of *The Washington Post* asserted that prison rape occurs because of "jails designed by an idiot so that the guards cannot see into the cells"[61] Along the same line, *The Los Angeles Times* noted that "[r]apes go on while deputies are nearby, but they can't hear because of the noise levels and couldn't see because of the blind spots."[62]

Blaming the Public

Although it was an infrequently deployed script, blaming the public for the problem of prison rape was not an altogether unvoiced perspective in news articles published during this time period. Among the articles that made some allusion to the public's culpability, attributions of blame varied in a number of ways. Some articles, for example, pointed a finger at a public that was aware of, but remained apathetic about, conditions in U.S. carceral facilities. In *The Chicago Daily Defender*, Senator Thomas J. Dodd (D-Conn.), Chairman of the Senate juvenile delinquency subcommittee, asserted in 1969 that "public and private apathy" about the "[a]bominable conditions [namely, prison rape] in U.S. prisons must be overcome so institutions can rehabilitate youthful offenders rather than turning them into hardened criminals."[63] The following year, the Oil City-Franklin-Clarion, Pennsylvania *Derrick* reported, "Because inmates seem to present no clear danger to society, the response to their needs may be one of indifference."[64] While this sentiment was infrequently expressed, such reports are notable in that they are the first to suggest that the public might share some of the culpability for the "abominations" occurring at the jails and prisons operating directly under its nose.

In contrast to scripts blaming public apathy, other articles suggested that the public ignorance of the problem was partly to blame. The notion that the public was unaware of the horrors occurring behind carceral walls was expressed in first in 1982 in *The Washington Post*. "[T]he rapes continue, hidden from public view yet with serious consequences to society," *The Post* warned.[65] Several months later, *The Post* suggested that the public *had been* ignorant of what was occurring in local jails but that the situation had been remedied, at least in Prince William County, Virginia. In an article reporting on the approval of a local bond issue to relieve overcrowding in Virginia jails, Circuit Court Judge Vincent Femia noted in *The Post* that the bond's passage "proves that once people know what's going on, they'll do what's necessary to stop sexual assaults. Getting the jail built will stop all that nonsense."[66] Like Reverend Louis Dwight's famous declaration, "When I shall bring before the Church of Christ a statement of what my eyes have seen, there will be a united and powerful effort to alleviate the miseries of Prisons,"[67] Judge Femia's statement paints a portrait of a well-intentioned but ignorant public, which – once made aware of the problem – would take whatever action necessary to remedy it.

Blaming "Types" of Prisoners

Although prison rape was not introduced to newspaper readers until 1969, other print media outlets had not remained entirely silent on the topic. A number of news and entertainment magazines – most notably *The Saturday Evening Post* – had begun to discuss sexual assault in U.S. prisons as early as the 1950s, principally in the context of a broader discourse about growing violence in carceral facilities across the nation. In the context of these early mid-century magazine articles, much of the blame for the proliferation of prison violence in general – and sexual assaults in particular – was attributed to a notoriously troublesome type of inmate, the "homosexual" prisoner.

Like homosexuals elsewhere, at mid-century, the incarcerated homosexual was represented in the media as a "sick," "wicked," "foul," "pathetic," "brutal" creature,[68] "suffering from some sort of personality disorder."[69] These individuals, along with certain other hopeless psychopaths incarcerated in American jails and prisons, were among the few prisoners whose innately violent and incorrigible nature rendered them beyond redemption. As Warden Baldi remarked in "What I've Learned About Convicts," a mid-century *Saturday Evening Post* article, the homosexual prisoner was understood to "have far less shame about [his] acts than do most other prisoners [and, therefore,] rehabilitation is seen as far less likely."[70]

John Martin's 1953 description of riots at the Michigan State Prison at Jackson, published in the *Saturday Evening Post*, was among the first to explicitly draw a connection between homosexual prisoners and the violence – sexual and otherwise – occurring in American prisons. In "Why Did It Happen, Part III" Martin described "wolf packs of homosexuals...prowl[ing] the cells blocks...raping and beating other inmates."[71] Similarly, Warden William H. Carty of New Jersey State Prison noted in *Collier's* that prison riots result in "waves of homosexual stabbings, and suicides are often caused by homosexuals as well." Indeed, in this 1954 article, Carty claimed, "90% of the murders and stabbings inside prison walls can be traced to homosexuals."[72]

Thus, by the time prison rape was introduced to the newspaper-reading public in 1969, the connection between homosexuality and prison violence was already well established in the print media and in the popular imagination. News journalists were quick to adopt and deploy this "violent homosexual" script in articles pertaining to sexual assault in U.S. jails and prisons. Throughout this time period, newspaper articles on prison rape commonly represented "homosexuality" as a "rampant"[73] and "massive evil"[74] of "epidemic proportions"[75] in American carceral facilities.

That homosexuality in prisons was a concern in and of itself is illustrated by the 1969 comments of Clinton T. Duffy. Quoted in the Hagerstown, Maryland *Daily Mail*, Duffy – generally considered one of the most liberal of the wardens to speak in this era – noted that "'one of the worst tragedies of prison life is the not infrequent transformation from heterosexual to homosexual preferences. Many of these men become so used to a male sex partner that they can't resume a normal relationship when the time comes.'" [76] Thus construed by this acknowledged authority, homosexuality in prison came to be understood as an aberration born of heterosexual deprivation – albeit one from which prisoners frequently do not recover.

More to the point in a discussion of prison rape, however, is Duffy's subsequent observation in *The Daily Mail* article cited above. "Homosexuality," Duffy claimed, is responsible for "nine-tenths of the nation's prison unrest."[77] As in Duffy's remark, throughout this time period "homosexuality" continued to be cited in the print news media as a root cause of prison violence. Indeed, the historical-era press frequently conflated homosexuality with violent behavior, using terms such as "homosexual rape," "homosexual stabbings," "homosexual violence" or "homosexual attack." One 1977 article in the *New York Times*, for example, links "homosexual rape" to "much of the 'inexplicable' violence nurtured in our 'correctional' facilities."[78]

While many articles about sexual violence in prisons deployed a "homosexuality" script in discussing prison rape, in contrast to the mid-century magazine articles described previously, by 1969 the use of the term "homosexual," if not its implication of incorrigibility and hopeless criminality, had begun to shift. By 1969, the term was used less to denote an innate psycho-sexual identity and more to connote a particular type of violent behavior.[79] That is, when the homosexual script was deployed, the discussion was far more likely to focus on sexual terrorism and the violence implied by rape than on the psycho-sexual orientation of the individuals involved. Understood in terms of the pragmatics of prison rape control, homosexuality came to represent a behavior engaged in by a particularly violent and incorrigible type of prisoner rather than a specific sexual identity.

A 1972 news article illuminates the growing tension between the notion of prison rape as "homosexuality" and prison rape as an act of power. "'Rule of Strong' in Prisons," which appeared in the September 18, 1972 edition of the Newark, Ohio *Advocate*, identifies "homosexuality" *and* "the rule of the strong over the weak" as co-culprits behind a homicide that occurred at Ohio State Penitentiary.[80] In contrast, a number of later articles begin to draw a more clear distinction between "homosexuality" and the violence of prison rape. A May 11, 1975 article in the *Pacific Stars and Stripes*, for example, states:

> Sexual relationships in prison are prompted by far more than sexual hunger. "Power is the essential motivation for prison rape…It is an act of domination.' As one 24-year-old former prisoner tells it: "You've got known homosexuals walking out in the yard – yet you have rape of young, innocent kids as well as older men. If it's sex they want, they could have gone after the homosexuals. The rapists are acting out their violence."[81]

A 1977 article in the New York Times provides a similar perspective on prison rape:

> In public forums, inmates who have participated in these assaults, as victims or victimizers, have quickly agreed on one major point: To label these attacks as "homosexual rape" is to ignore what is happening. One ex-offender called attacks "power plays."[82]

Not uncommonly, news articles published in the historical period blamed "homosexuality" for the problem of sexual violence in prisons. Prior to the midpoint of the period, about half of the articles published assigned at least part of the blame for the problem to "homosexuals" or "homosexuality." Although it amounted to a dominant discourse throughout the first half of the historical era, the script blaming prison rape on "homosexuals" and "homosexuality" declined dramatically as the 1970s drew to a close and it all but disappeared from news articles published after 1981.

As homosexual prisoners were increasingly reimagined as victims rather than predators, a new "type" of prisoner emerged to take the place of the homosexual as the quintessential prison rapist. In the latter half of the historical period, African-American prisoners were increasingly represented in the press – albeit in various and sometimes subtle ways – as the culprits responsible for the problem of prison rape. Reporting on Senate juvenile delinquency subcommittee hearings on rape in U.S. prisons, a March 4, 1969 story published in the *Chicago Daily Defender* was among the first to introduce prison rape to the news-reading public. The *Daily Defender* article began by introducing the reader to "John Doe," a prisoner reportedly selected by computer "as typical of the thousands faced by corrections officials every year." Doe had been brought from his cell in a Washington, D.C. jail to testify before the Senate subcommittee on juvenile delinquency.

A 25-year-old, "heavy set Negro," "in and out of jail since [the age of] 16," and a "drug addict," Doe had reportedly been jailed for the past five months while awaiting trial on a weapons charge, his sixth felony offense. The exact nature of Doe's contribution to the hearings was not specified in the *Daily Defender* article. However, his description, coupled with a relatively large photo of the reputedly incorrigible black prisoner in chains, seems to speak for itself. While not overtly identified as a prison rapist, this "typical prisoner" sat in clear contrast to the youthful, fundamentally redeemable offender – and potential prison rape victim – that constituted the primary concern of the subcommittee's investigation.

More subtly, in the Tofani narrative discussed earlier, the rapist's blackness was communicated by virtue of a regrettable childhood spent in Capitol Heights, a notoriously poor, crime-plagued, and homogeneously African-American neighborhood in the shadow of the U.S. capitol building. Similarly, a September 1969 article in the Hagerstown *Daily Mail* referred to a "dangerous" section of a local prison where rape is commonplace as "the jungle," clearly a reference to the African-American heritage of the inmates housed there.

A number of later articles blatantly identify aggressors and victims by race. *The Progress-Index,* an Indianapolis, Indiana newspaper, reported the rape of a youthful and obviously white inmate in a New Jersey facility:

> A 19-year-old inmate at the Petersburg Federal Reformatory was freed this week after the youth claimed he had been raped by three other prisoners. Jan Elgaard of Ramsey, N.J....was given a rehabilitative sentence under the Youthful Offenders Act, which is designed to help young first-time wrongdoers solve personality problems which led them to crime. Lawyers for the youth charged last month that Elgaard was awakened in his cell at 2 a.m. Feb. 28 and raped by three black inmates who threatened to kill him if he did not submit.[83]

No small number of articles reporting on efforts by inmates at Rahway Prison in New Jersey to scare potential juvenile defenders straight featured wire-service photos of menacing black figures in prison garb looming over a dozen-or-so frightened juveniles. The prisoners' message to the group of delinquents amounts to a graphic description of prison sexual violence intended to scared the budding criminals straight. At the same time, it points the finger of blame at the amoral, incorrigible, and by now iconic African American rapist:

> We got a lot of niggers in here...who like that ass. They don't have no connection with no bitch. So they result with young boys like you. These niggers going to take advantage of you, because they ain't never going to have a woman again. You'll be f-----.[84]

Over the entire course of the historical period, more than 40% of articles published deployed a script implicitly or explicitly blaming African-American, or at least not-white, prisoners for the problem of prison rape. Interestingly, articles blaming non-whites for prison rape were most prevalent between 1975 and 1985, comprising nearly 60% of the articles published during that ten-year time span. After 1985, the number of articles blaming non-whites declined to about 50% and remained at that level across the remainder of the historical period. In this context, it is interesting to note that prison rapists were *never* identified by race unless they were identified as African-American or at least "not white." Not one article published during this time period identified a prison rapist as a white prisoner.

During the historical era (1969-2006), the vast majority of prison rape-related articles published in U.S. newspapers framed the subject within a larger discourse about institutional failure – specifically, the failure of the U.S. prison system.   Articles that employed this diagnostic frame deployed a variety of not unrelated scripts, constituting sexual violence in carceral facilities as a symptom of U.S. prisons' fundamental malignancy and/or an indication of prisons' failure on specific, mandated dimensions of correctional performance, including controlling and rehabilitating offenders and protecting the safety of the community outside prison walls.   These scripts were neither contradictory nor mutually exclusive and articles framing prison rape as a symptom of institutional failure frequently drew on two or more of them to illustrate the connection between prison rape and the failure of U.S. corrections.. Thus, while there may have been little agreement about where exactly to place the locus of blame for the problem, there appears to have been considerable consensus among members of the historical-era press that prison rape represented a serious social problem in need of a solution. On the other hand, the sudden, marked decline in the volume of news media discourse on the subject during the second half of the historical era may indicate that such a conclusion is not entirely accurate. Indeed, the dramatic drop in the volume of prison-rape related news articles may reflect an ideological shift as well as a quantitative one. That is, the absence of news media discourse about prison rape during the latter years of the historical era may not be unrelated to a number of cultural shifts that were occurring contemporaneously.

---

[1] MacCormick, Austin. "Behind Those Prison Riots." *Reader's Digest*. December 1953: 97-101.

[2] "Prisoners On Strike: The Meaning. *U.S. News and World Report*. May 2, 1952: 20-21.

[3] "Why Convicts Riot." *U.S. News and World Report*. December 19, 1952: 18-21.

[4] Wilson, Donald Powell and Harry Elmore Barnes. "Riot is an Unnecessary Evil." *Life*. November 24, 1952: 71-72.

[5] "Evidence of Homosexual Rape Found in Philadelphia Jails." *The Ruston Daily Leader*. March 27, 1969

[6] "De Profundis." *The Derrick*, Oil City-Franklin-Clarion, Pennsylvania. March 9, 1970.

[7] "De Profundis." *The Register*, Danville Virginia. April 4, 1969.

[8] "Sexual Abuse of Inmates Bared in Senate." *The Chicago Daily Defender*. March 4, 1969.

[9] "Evidence of Homosexual Rape Found in Philadelphia Jails." *The Ruston Daily Leader*. March 27, 1969; "Administration Terms Report 'Sensational.'" *The Pharos-Tribune & Press*, Logansport, Indiana. March 26, 1969.

[10] "Terror Behind Bars." *The Washington Post*. September 26, 1982.

[11] "He Prefers Death to Florida Prison." *The Times Record*, Troy, New York. February 27, 1975.

[12] "Rape Threat Held Valid Reason for Escape from Jail." *The New York Times*. January 20, 1975.

[13] "Sexual Abuse Of Inmates Bared in Senate." *The Chicago Daily Defender*. March 4, 1969.

[14] "*De Profundis.*" *The Register*, Danville, Virginia. April 4, 1969.

[15] "Crisis in the Prisons: Not Enough Room for All the Criminals." *U.S. News and World Report*. November 28, 1977.

[16] "American Penology Failure: Jail At the Lower Level of Penal System is Weak Link." *The Derrick*, Oil City-Franklin-Clarion, Pennsylvania. March 9, 1970.

[17] "Crisis in the Prisons: Not Enough Room for All the Criminals." *U.S. News and World Report*. November 28, 1977.

[18] "*De Profundis.*" *The Register*, Danville, Virginia. April 4, 1969.

[19] "Crisis in the Prisons: Not Enough Room for All the Criminals." *U.S. News and World Report*. November 28, 1977.

[20] "*De Profundis.*" *The Register*, Danville, Virginia. April 4, 1969.

[21] "Administration Terms Report 'Sensational.'" *The Pharos-Tribune & Press*, Logansport, Indiana. March 26, 1969.

[22] "As if Imprisonment Is Not Enough." *The New York Times*. January 29, 1977.

[23] "Justice May Not Be Served." *The Washington Post*. September 27, 1982.

[24] "Terror Behind Bars." *The Washington Post*. September 26, 1982.

[25] "Religious Magazines Look at U.S. Prisons." *The Daily Mail*, Hagerstown, Maryland. September 13, 1969.

[26] "Sexual Abuse of Inmates Bared in Senate." *The Chicago Daily Defender.* March 4, 1969.

[27] "American Penology Failure: Jail At the Lower Level of Penal System is Weak Link." *The Derrick,* Oil City-Franklin-Clarion, Pennsylvania. March 9, 1970.

[28] "The Strong Inmates Exploit the Weak." *The Washington Post.* September 28, 1982.

[29] "Rape Is the Way Some Master the Violent Art of Jail Survival." *The Washington Post.* September 28, 1982.

[30] Terror Behind Bars." *The Washington Post.* September 26, 1982.

[31] "Justice May Not Be Served." *The Washington Post.* September 27, 1982.

[32] "Pulls No Punches, Bleeps No Words: Scared Straight Brutal Reality." *The Boston Globe.* February 23, 1979.

[33] Ibid.

[34] "'Scared Straight,' Will It Work Here?" *The Washington Post.* March 23, 1979.

[35] "Cons Tell Juveniles About Life in Prison." *The Evening Capital,* Annapolis, Maryland. March 23, 1979.

[36] "'Scared Straight,' Will It Work Here?" *The Washington Post.* March 23, 1979.

[37] "Man Becomes Prison Expert Behind Bars." *The Capital Times,* Lansing, Michigan. September 26, 1974.

[38] "The Jailer." *The Washington Post.* September 26, 1982.

[39] "De Profundis." *The Register,* Danville, Virginia. April 4, 1969.

[40] "Evidence of Homosexual Rape Found in Philadelphia Jails." *The Ruston Daily Leader.* March 27, 1969; see also, "Administration Terms Report 'Sensational.'" *The Pharos-Tribune & Press,* Logansport, Indiana. March 26, 1969; "Religious Magazines Look at U.S. Prisons." *The Daily Mail,* Hagerstown, Maryland. September 13, 1969.

[41] The Associated Press. Domestic News. Dateline: Detroit. September 11, 1979.

[42] The Associated Press. Domestic News. Dateline: Richmond, Virginia. October 23, 1979.

[43] It is interesting to note that, although the various judgments mentioned were intended to compensate victims for "civil rights" violations, the press almost studiously avoided saying so. Articles that mentioned financial remunerations awarded to raped prisoners most commonly indicated that these awards constituted compensation for correctional "negligence" or simply "damages."

Only one article published during this entire time period indicated that an inmate had been awarded compensation for "civil rights violations" (The Associated Press. Domestic News. Dateline: Detroit. September 11, 1979).
[44] "High Court Weighs Guard Liability." *The Washington Post*. November 11, 1982.
[45] "As If Imprisonment Itself Is Not Horrendous Enough..." *The New York Times*. January 29, 1977.
[46] Ibid.
[47] "Punishment." *The Washington Post*. September 28, 1982.
[48] "Ex-POW's Testimony Caps Suit Over Conditions in Jail." *The Los Angeles Times*. May 1, 1980.
[49] Although they were not portrayed as entirely without fault, correctional officers were conspicuous in their absence from the list of those believed to be perpetrating sexual assaults within carceral walls. While correctional officers were depicted as reprehensible for neglecting their duty to protect inmates in their charge, and potentially liable for that neglect in a court of law, they were never mentioned as perpetrators of sexual assaults during this period.
[50] "Punishment." *The Washington Post*. September 28, 1982.
[51] "Terror Behind Bars." *The Washington Post*. September 26, 1982.
[52] "Evidence of Homosexual Rape Found in Philadelphia Jails." *The Ruston Daily Leader*. March 27, 1969.
[53] "Ex-POW's Testimony Caps Suit Over Conditions in Jail." *The Los Angeles Times*. May 1, 1980.
[54] "De Profundis." *The Register*, Danville, Virginia. April 4, 1969.
[55] "He Prefers Death to Florida Prison." *The Times Record*, Troy, New York. February 27, 1975.
[56] "American Penology Failure: Jail At Lower Level of Penal System is Weak Link." *The Derrick*, Oil City-Franklin-Clarion, Pennsylvania. March 9, 1970.
[57] "Ex-POW's Testimony Caps Suit Over Conditions in Jail." *The Los Angeles Times*. May 1, 1980.
[58] "Prince George's Jail Bond Issue Passes: $20 Million Approved for New Facility." *The Washington Post*. November 3, 1982.
[59] "De Profundis." *The Register*, Danville, Virginia. April 4, 1969.
[60] "American Penology Failure: Jail At Lower Level of Penal System is Weak Link." *The Derrick*, Oil City-Franklin-Clarion, Pennsylvania. March 9, 1970.
[61] "Punishment." *The Washington Post*. September 28, 1982.
[62] "Ex-POW's Testimony Caps Suit Over Conditions in Jail." *The Los Angeles Times*. May 1, 1980.

[63] "Sexual Abuse of Inmates Bared in Senate." *The Washington Post*. March 4, 1969.

[64] "American Penology Failure: Jail At the Lower Level of Penal System is Weak Link." *The Derrick*, Oil City-Franklin-Clarion, Pennsylvania. March 9, 1970.

[65] "The Strong Inmates Exploit the Weak." *The Washington Post*. September 28, 1982.

[66] "Prince George's Jail Bond Issue Passes: $20 Million Approved for New Facility." *The Washington Post*. November 3, 1982.

[67] *Reports of the Prison Discipline Society of Boston*. 1972. (Publication No. 155: Reprint Series in Criminology, Law Enforcement, and Social Problems). Patterson Smith: Montclair, New Jersey.

[68] Shelly, Gordon and David Mazaroff. "Draughts of Old Bourbon." *American Mercury*. June 1952: 118-25.

[69] Duffy, Clinton T. "San Quentin is My Home, Part Five." *The Saturday Evening Post*. April 22, 1950: 134-136.

[70] Baldi, Frederick S. "What I've Learned About Convicts, Part I." *The Saturday Evening Post*. September 5, 1953: 17-19, 52-54.

[71] Martin, John Bartlow. "Why Did It Happen: The Riot at Jackson Prison, Part III." *The Saturday Evening Post*. June 20, 1953: 36-37, 62-67.

[72] Carty, William H. "You've Got to Be Tougher than the Toughs." *Collier's*. March 5, 1954: 70-75.

[73] "Sexual Abuse of Inmates Bared in Senate." *Chicago Daily Defender*. March 4, 1969.

[74] "Administration Terms Report Sensational." *The Pharos-Tribune & Press*. March 26, 1969; and "Evidence of Homosexual Rape Found in Philadelphia Jails." *The Ruston Daily Leader*. March 27, 1969.

[75] "Vivid Expose on Prison Rape." *Pacific Stars and Stripes*. May 11, 1975.

[76] "Religious Magazines Look at U.S. Prisons." *The Daily Mail*, Hagerstown, Maryland. September 13, 1969.

[77] Ibid.

[78] "As If Imprisonment Itself Is Not Enough." *New York Times*. January 29. 1977.

[79] It is particularly interesting to note that the term "homosexual" was *never* used as a noun in the newspaper articles that constituted the data set for this research. "Homosexuality" was used instead, but the term was used in reference to a behavior not a sexual identity.

[80] In this instance, an inmate killed another prisoner when the latter made overt sexual advances toward the former's cellmate.

[81] "And Nothing is Done About It : Vivid Exposé on Prison Rape." *Pacific Stars & Stripes.* May 11, 1975.

[82] "As If Imprisonment Itself Is Not Horrendous Enough." *The New York Times.* January 29, 1977.

[83] "Reformatory Inmate Freed After Alleged Prison Rape." *The Progress-Index,* Indianapolis, Indiana. March 19, 1976.

[84] "Cons Tell Juveniles About Life in Prison." *The Evening Capital,* Annapolis, Maryland. March 23, 1979.

CHAPTER THREE

Prison Rape in the Popular Press, 1992-2006

INTRODUCTION

In the wake of the social upheaval and political unrest that characterized the American scene during the turbulent 1960s, by the 1970s the nation struggled to reconstitute the role of a strong central government. One method of achieving this goal was to mount a visible tough-on-crime campaign. The Nixon-era criminal justice buildup – a wave of law-and-order politics and policies that swept the nation in the 1970s – was an attempt to re-engineer a socio-economic system in crisis (Parenti 1999). This policy shift did not immediately translate into higher rates of incarceration. However, in conjunction with the Regan-era war on drugs, by the early 1980s rates of imprisonment in the U.S. began to surge. Between 1980 and 1994, the incarcerated population in the U.S. increased by 300%, from 500,000 to 1.5 million and estimates indicate that federal, state, and local expenditure for corrections by this time had reached $30 billion, "up from $4 billion in 1975" (Beckett 1997: 89).

The increase in the number of persons held in federal, state, and local facilities was accompanied by dramatic changes in the composition of the incarcerated population. While counts earlier in the century had placed the proportion of black prisoners at 22%, by 1992 African-Americans amounted to 51% of the entire prison population, a change primarily traceable to the effects of the war on drugs (Beckett 1997). As Beckett (1997:89) points out, once the war on drugs was underway "90% of those admitted to prison for drug offenses were black or Hispanic." Similarly, Regan-era drug policies led to an enormous surge in the number of women incarcerated in state prisons. The number of women imprisoned for drug offenses increased by 828% between 1986 and 1991 (Beckett 1996).

As the nation shifted toward the political right during the 1980s, even liberals became more conservative, especially with regard to the treatment of suspected and convicted lawbreakers (Welch 1996). A result of these changes was the increasing popularity of a "just-deserts" model of criminal justice policy, promoted by liberals and conservatives alike (Sloop 1996). According to the tenets of this model, criminals should be given only their due, nothing more and nothing less. From this perspective, every criminal activity entails a specific measure of punishment and the distribution of that punishment is the sole responsibility of the criminal justice system in its relationship with criminals. Other considerations, such as rehabilitation or training are not required. However, they may be offered on a voluntary basis. "While prisoners should be provided with clean cells that allow them to maintain a sense of humanity, and while rehabilitation programs should be available for those prisoners who volunteer to take part in them, undergoing the prescribed punishment is the only necessary concern of criminal justice" (Sloop 1996:133). As one key advocate explained, the just-deserts model advocates a return to retribution, but with an emphasis on fairness (Fogel 1979). Accordingly, the goal of imprisonment is to be humane, not excessively painful, and prisoners' constitutional rights are to be protected above all else.

A factor that contributed to the rise and success of the just deserts model was a notable drop in society's faith in the viability of rehabilitation as a goal of incarceration. In 1974, Lipton, Martinson and Wilks published a meta-analysis assessing all the evaluations of criminal rehabilitation programs between 1945 and 1967. Their now famous – or to many infamous – report concluded that, "With few and isolated exceptions, the rehabilitative efforts that have been reported so far have had no appreciable effect on recidivism." [1] In short, the authors concluded, when it comes to rehabilitating prisoners no one program is better than another and, at the end of the day, *nothing works.* The notoriety of this position was increased far beyond the scholarly and correctional community, particularly through the efforts of Martinson, whose flamboyant personality largely eclipsed the participation of his co-authors. In widely read essays on the purpose of punishment written for *Newsweek*,[2] and *Public Interest*,[3] Martinson claimed that large scale rehabilitation of prisoners is, in a word, infeasible. His views were embraced by the corrections industry and the press alike such that, by the early 1990s Martinson's "nothing works" position was taken as axiomatic among correctional professionals and much of the public as well.

In addition, by the 1990s sexual misconduct on the part of correctional had staff emerged as a topic of concern for corrections officials and an object of interest in the press. Although staff-on-inmate sexual misconduct was neither illegal nor criminal in most jurisdictions until the latter decades of the twentieth century, by 1996, the U.S. Congress and more than half of U.S. state legislatures had passed laws defining sexual misconduct by correctional staff as a criminal offense. A majority of this legislative activity had taken place over the first four to five years of the 1990s. One result of state and federal-level legislative activity reconstituting staff-on-inmate sexual contact as a crime was a marked increase in individual and class action suits based on allegations of sexual misconduct filed against various departments of corrections since 1990. According to the National Institute of Corrections (NIC), in the early 1990s approximately half of all Departments of Corrections in the U.S. had been party to litigation stemming from staff-on-inmate sexual misconduct allegations. By 1996, 19 of the 53 reporting correctional jurisdictions were embroiled in litigation related to sexual misconduct and, of those 19, five had been involved in other similar litigation during the preceding five-year period. An additional five DOCs that were not actively responding to such litigation in 1996 had been involved in such suits at some point during that same period. Judgments in a number of class action suits favored the plaintiffs and were resolved through the consent decrees designed to remedy institutional deficiencies that, the courts opined, amounted to unconstitutional conditions of confinement.

Ultimately, concern over the volume of prisoner-generated litigation occupying the courts led to legislative intervention in the form of the Prison Litigation Reform Act of 1995 (PLRA).[4] Originally passed by Congress as a way to stem the tide against what were thought to be frivolous lawsuits by prisoners, the law has since been used repeatedly to limit prisoners' access to the courts.   The PLRA has many provisions. Among the most important are the requirements that prisoners exhaust all administrative remedies provided for their grievance prior to filing suit in federal court. Those who fail to take their complaints through every level of a prison's grievance procedure almost certainly see their suits dismissed by the court. Creating a particular burden for many victims of prison rape, the Act also contained a provision barring prisoners from bringing federal action for "mental or emotional injury suffered while in custody without a prior showing of physical injury."[5]

By the 1990s, a number of human rights organizations had begun to take up the issue of custodial rape. Stop Prisoner Rape (SPR), for example, was originally founded as "People Organized to Stop Rape of Imprisoned Persons" (POSRIP) by rape survivor Russell Dan Smith in 1980. By 1994, the organization was incorporated as Stop Prisoner Rape by Stephen Donaldson, also a survivor of prison rape. As the second leader of SPR, Donaldson wrote articles and editorials on prison sexual assault, was featured in elite media outlets, coordinated SPR's amicus brief for the landmark legal case on prisoner rape, *Farmer v. Brennan* (1994, and launched SPR's high profile website. Two survivors of sexual assault, Don Collins and Tom Cahill, followed Donaldson as the leader of SPR until 2001 when the group opened its first permanent office and hired Lara Stemple as Executive Director. This marked the first time the leader of SPR was not a survivor of prison sexual assault and, importantly, it put a lawyer and legal scholar with a background in human rights at the helm of SPR. Thereafter, SPR became a driving force behind the move to pass legislation aimed at reducing or eliminating prison rape in U.S. carceral facilities.

Like SPR, Human Rights Watch (HRW) took up the cause of rape in U.S. carceral facilities. In December 1996, HRW released *All Too Familiar: Sexual Abuse of Women in U.S. State Prisons*, a report documenting pervasive sexual harassment, sexual abuse, and privacy violations by guards and other corrections department employees in state prisons in California, the District of Columbia, Georgia, Illinois, Michigan, and New York. The report also exposed the failure of states to respond to women's reports of sexual abuse and harassment. This report was followed by *Nowhere to Hide: Retaliation Against Women in Michigan State Prisons* in 1998 and, in April of 2001, HRW released a report called *No Escape: Male Rape in U.S. Prison*. This report, written by Joanne Mariner, contained dozens of first-hand accounts of prisoner rape and sexual assault, stories considered both horrifying and sobering.

In addition to the efforts of SPR and HRW, various bodies working under the auspices of the United Nations High Commissioner for Human Rights were instrumental in focusing international attention on rape of incarcerated and detained individuals (e.g., The Committee Against Torture (the body of independent experts monitoring implementation of the Convention against Torture and Other Cruel, Inhuman or Degrading Treatment or Punishment by its State parties), the UN Special Rapporteur on torture, and the UN Special Rapporteur on violence against women). In 1992, the UN Special Rapporteur on Torture declared: "it was clear that rape or other forms of sexual assault . . . in detention were a particularly ignominious violation of the inherent dignity and right to physical integrity of the human being and, accordingly, they constitute an act of torture" (Summary Record of 21st Meeting, U.N. ESCOR, Comm'n Hum. Rts, 48th Sess., para 35, U.N. Doc. E/CN.4/1992/SR.21, 1992).

In 1998, Ms. Radhika Coomaraswamy, the U.N. Special Rapporteur on violence against women, its causes, and consequences, visited Washington D.C. and the states of New York, Connecticut, New Jersey, Georgia, California, Michigan and Minnesota to study the issue of violence against women in the state and federal prisons in each of the states mentioned. Wherever the Special Rapporteur went, officials asked her why she decided to visit the United States. She explained that based on information received from diverse sources, she was convinced that there were serious issues of custodial sexual misconduct in United States prisons that had to be investigated. "Although the United States has a comparatively high level of political freedom," the Special Rapporteur asserted, "some aspects of its criminal justice system pose fundamental human rights questions. Other special rapporteurs have also stressed this point."[6]

Following her visit to the United States, the Special Rapporteur issued a mixed but nonetheless scathing report regarding the treatment of women in U.S. carceral facilities. The report covered a number of issues that were of concern to the U.N., including racial and gender disparities among carceral populations in the U.S., impunity of corrections officers, and sexual misconduct of officers in U.S. women's prisons. In the context of her report, Ms. Coomaraswamy asserted,

"[I]t is clear that sexual misconduct by male corrections officers against women inmates is widespread."[7]

In addition to the above-mentioned issues, the late 1980s and the 1990s witnessed a growing national awareness of the AIDS epidemic in general and the disproportionately high incidence of AIDS among carceral populations in particular. As an April 1998 article posted to the world-wide web stated:

> Prisons and jails contain perhaps the highest concentrations of persons infected with HIV and those at greatest risk of acquiring HIV by injection drug use and sexual contact. According to a report by the US Bureau of Justice Statistics, the rate of confirmed AIDS cases is more than six times higher in state and federal prisons than in the general population. About 2.3 percent of all persons incarcerated in the US in 1995 were HIV-seropositive, and about 0.51 percent had confirmed AIDS.[8]

That AIDS among carceral populations was a concern among the general public was confirmed by a 1994 *Boston Globe* survey which indicated that while only 63% of respondents considered prison rape to be a cause for concern, 85% of people surveyed said they were concerned about the issue of prison rape in light of AIDS.[9] On June 12, 1994, *The Globe* noted that sexual assaults in prisons "are not just grotesque add-on penalties but death sentences. The percentage of inmates infected with the AIDS virus is now 14 times as high as in the population at large."[10]

In contrast to the sporadic and relatively low level of discourse about prison rape in the print news media prior to 1992, subsequent years witnessed a marked increase in number of articles on the subject published in the American press. For example, the 15-year period from 1992 through 2006 saw a total of 298 articles pertaining to prison rape published in elite and popular U.S. newspapers – nearly six times the total articles published during the preceding 23-year period and a ten-fold increase over the annual average for the preceding period. Although the quantity of articles fluctuated from year to year, the general increase was sustained and in fact became more pronounced over time.

The increase in the volume of discourse about prison rape in the contemporary era media was accompanied by discernable shifts in its content. Analysis of data presented in Chapter 2 revealed that, in the historical era, prison rape was framed almost exclusively within a discourse about institutional failure – specifically, the failure of a dysfunctional and ultimately malignant U.S. prison system. By 1992, however, the penchant for employing an institutional failure frame declined and, by 1995, that construction had all but disappeared. Indeed, by the middle of the decade, new ways of framing the problem had emerged and, over time, became the dominant representations of prison rape in the contemporary print news media.

DIAGNOSING THE PROBLEM

Rights

Notwithstanding the judiciary's massive, mid-century intervention into the governance of U.S. prisons (Feeley & Rubin, 1998) and the courts' reconstitution of the American prisoner as rights-bearing citizen, historically, the media had effectively left any connection between prison rape and "rights" unarticulated. After 1992, however, the contemporary era press increasingly came to frame prison rape as a rights issue. Indeed, nearly 65% of contemporary-era articles framed prison rape first and foremost as a rights-related problem. Emerging in conjunction with the torrent of corrections-related legal actions flooding the courts, as well as growing concern about carceral rape among human rights advocacy groups, prison rape framed as a rights issue rapidly came to dominate the discourse in the contemporary-era print news media.

Constitutional Rights

Despite a succession of appellate-level court decisions limiting the extent to which correctional systems and officials could be held liable for the safety and well-being of prisoners, the 1990s witnessed a dramatic increase in prisoner-generated legal actions alleging injuries that implicated the Eighth Amendment ban on cruel and unusual punishments. Media attention to the plethora of rights-related cases that packed the calendars in U.S. courtrooms accounted for a substantial portion of the articles that framed prison rape as a rights issue. Of the articles that framed prison rape in these terms, about 39% deployed a script representing sexual violence in prisons as an issue that implicated prisoners' constitutional rights.

Newspaper articles that deployed the "constitutional rights" script showcased the courts' ongoing efforts to define and delimit the rights extended to prisoners under the provisions of the U.S. Constitution. The 1994 case of *Farmer v. Brennan*, which established the current standard for determining correctional liability in cases of prison rape, received extensive coverage in U.S. newspapers. An article published in the Memphis, Tennessee *Commercial Appeal* is typical of many that endeavored to make sense of *Farmer v. Brennan* (1994) for the news-reading public. Titled "Court Hears Lawsuit from Transsexual in Prison Rape Case," the article reported:

> The Clinton administration and a transsexual inmate allegedly raped in federal prison clashed Wednesday in a Supreme Court showdown over prison officials' duty to protect one inmate from another. Raped inmates should not collect monetary damages from prison officials unless the officials reacted with "deliberate indifference" to "a considerable risk...not just the normal risk of being in prison...Farmer, 27, has the appearance and demeanor of a woman, enhanced by silicone breast implants and female hormones. But Farmer has male organs...Now in prison in Florence, Colo., Farmer has been diagnosed as HIV-positive, carrying the human immunodeficiency virus that causes AIDS.[11]

In similar terms, a June 7, 1994 article in *The Chicago Sun-Times* reported on the Court's decision in *Farmer v. Brennan*:

> The Supreme Court on Monday unanimously reinstated a case brought by a transsexual who was raped in prison, but ruled that prison officials are liable for injuries only if they actually knew the risk an inmate faced and disregarded it....Dee Farmer, who is serving a 20-year sentence for credit card fraud, was born male but underwent estrogen therapy, had breast implants and, according to the court opinion, unsuccessful "black market" surgery to remove his testicles.

Farmer sued federal prison officials for confining him in 1989 with the general population at a Terre Haute, Ind., penitentiary. He alleges that it would have been clear to them that a transsexual "who projects feminine characteristics," would be particularly vulnerable to sexual attack.[12]

Also focusing on *Farmer v. Brennan, The Boston Globe* reported:

At issue in the case was the Eighth Amendment to the Constitution, which protects against cruel and unusual punishment...Legal specialists and inmate advocates views the ruling as a victory for inmates and anticipated that it would trigger a flood of lawsuits"[13]

Related, *The Chicago Sun-Times* noted, "[T]he opinion ultimately could allow more prisoners to get their grievances to trial at a time of increased crowding and prisons' inability to separate predators from victims."[14]

Implicit in many of the articles reporting on prison rape-related legal actions was at least some degree of ambivalence about the legitimacy of convicted criminals in the role of rights-claimers. Prisoners' allegations of sexual violence and the harm associated with it were juxtaposed in these articles with arguably irrelevant but nonetheless extensive, highly detailed accounts of the crimes for which plaintiffs were incarcerated, their prior convictions, and other potentially inflammatory details of their personal lives and criminal histories. Among the many accounts of proceedings in *Farmer v. Brennan* (1994), for example, few failed to devote a significant portion of the text to the gruesome details of the plaintiff's transsexuality, her positive HIV status, and her penchant for credit card fraud and illegal drug use.

The extent of damages awarded to plaintiffs who succeeded in stating valid Eighth Amendment claims was commonly the focus of attention in the press. Specific dollar equivalents were displayed prominently in the text of such articles and often appeared in their titles as well. Among the articles that relied on a constitutional rights script, almost 35% bore titles that included the specific dollar amount of damages stemming from incidents of sexual assault. Examples include articles like "Former Lamb County Inmate Awarded $287,500 in 1999

Jail Rape,"[15] "Federal Jury Awards $4 Million to Former Prisoner in Rape Case,"[16] "Former Inmate Files $6 Million Rape Lawsuit,"[17] "Fisher Sues for $20 Million Over Alleged Prison Rape,"[18] and "State Settles Prison Rape Charge for $36,000."[19] An article in the *St. Louis Post-Dispatch*, for example, noted:

> Lawyers representing Jefferson County, Sheriff Oliver "Glenn" Boyer, and others have agreed to offer a cash settlement to a woman who was raped in the county jail in Hillsboro after a male inmate was placed in her cell according to documents filed with a federal court in St. Louis…Attorneys involved in the case have two weeks to agree on the settlement's final dollar amount. But no matter the amount, the county won't have to pay out more than $5000, the county's insurance deductible, said Marc Fried.[20]

Similarly, an article in *The Palm Beach Post* reported on the case of an anonymous woman who was allegedly impregnated as a result of a sexual attack by a St. Lucie County, Florida corrections officer:

> The child she says is a product of an assault is now 3 years old, and the man she names as the father is on probation, but a state inmate filed a civil suit Dec. 7 for her alleged attack by a St. Lucie County corrections officer four years earlier. The 27-year-old woman remains in prison until 2020 on armed-robbery charges, and her little boy is cared for by a service similar to foster care…The woman seeks compensatory damages for the costs of raising a child and the emotional damage of the alleged rape. Johnson said those damages should exceed $100,000. Johnson said his client also seeks punitive damages, though he did not yet have a value.[21]

An article that appeared on February 7, 1992 in the *St. Louis Post-Dispatch* highlighted the apparent disconnect between the public's perception of prisoner's rights and that of the court. The *Post-Dispatch* reported on a federal appeals court decision remanding the case of four victims of prison rape for retrial. At issue was the compensation awarded to plaintiffs by the jury in a lower court. Having agreed that the plaintiffs had "recklessly been exposed to the pervasive risk of sexual assault," the jury awarded each prisoner only one dollar in damages, an amount the appellate court judged to be "shockingly inadequate."[22] According to the *Post-Dispatch*, the plaintiffs were prisoners convicted of child abuse, sodomy, and burglary. "The jury's reluctance to award adequate damages may well rest on prejudice against the plaintiffs as prisoners convicted of unsavory crimes," the article asserted.[23] Similarly, *The San Francisco Chronicle* reported on the settlement of a case involving the rape of an 18-year-old prisoner at the San Bruno jail. In addition to the $400,000 damages awarded to the plaintiff, San Francisco city officials had agreed to spend $4.5 million to make improvements aimed at curbing jail violence. In reaction, the Chronicle reported, "Now we're faced with diverting millions of dollars that are needed for the homeless, the Muni, libraries and other community programs and we're still not coming up with a long-term solution to the problem."[24]

Published in a number of major newspapers across the country, a series of eight Associated Press (AP) wire-service articles reported on the proceedings and outcome of a 1997 civil rights action filed by Illinois prisoner Michael E. Blucker. "Sentenced in 1993 to 10 years in prison for burglary, Blucker, 28...said he was raped repeatedly while an inmate at the Menard Correctional Center."[25] Blucker's case was sensational in that he claimed not only to have been raped but also "bought and sold by 'Gangster Disciples' gang members, who prostituted him and other inmates in exchange for drugs, alcohol, cigarettes and soap."[26] Blucker sued the Illinois Department of Corrections and a number of prison officials, claiming that his civil rights were violated by the "seven prison employees who remained 'deliberately indifferent' to the attacks."[27]

The ambivalence discernable in news media accounts of prison rape-related legal actions described above was apparent in the AP articles pertaining to Blucker's case as well. More than that, however, the two final articles in the series intimate that the failure of the plaintiff's Eighth Amendment claim was received as a welcome legal outcome. Indeed, the titles of the two final articles in the series, "No Award in Prison Rape Case!"[28] and "Jury Vindicates Guards in Prison Rape Case"[29] arguably convey a sense of relief and excited approval in regard to jurors' decision to absolve officers and prison officials of wrongdoing. In the end, the Associated Press reported, "the courtroom exploded with applause and shouts of joy" as the jury's findings were read. [30]

Human Rights

Alongside news media accounts that deployed a constitutional rights script, a second rights-related discourse emerged in the contemporary era. Depicting prison rape as a human rights issue, news articles that deployed this script universally expressed unmitigated concern about epidemic sexual violence U.S. carceral facilities and frequently included calls for popular and legislative action to stem the tide of epidemic rape in American prisons and jails. Articles drawing on a human rights script amounted to about 60% of the total articles published in the contemporary period and deployment of the script increased over time such that, during the latter half of the period, representation of prison rape as a human rights issue amounted to the dominant discourse on the subject published in elite and popular U.S. newspapers.

News reports that relied on a human rights script commonly took the form of exposés. Such articles often included victims' first person testimony which effectively personalized the physical harm of prison rape and its attendant psychological horrors. In addition, desperate pleas from the relatives of still-incarcerated rape victims along with graphic descriptions of classic prison rape scenarios were common components of articles that relied on the human rights script and notably, a significant number of these articles interjected the specter of AIDS contracted in prison – an unadjudicated "death sentence" – into the discussion about rape in U.S. carceral facilities.

A May 1, 1994 *Boston Globe* article is typical of this discourse:

> Medina's convictions last year: assault with a dangerous weapon. His sentence: a minimum of three years in state prison. But his punishment has gone far beyond that. Medina says he has been repeatedly raped in prison. Scrawny and baby-faced, his was a target the day he walked in. During his first month at the Massachusetts Correctional Institution at Shirley, he says, a cellmate nearly twice his size held a razor to his neck and raped him in their 6-by-8-foot cell. There were more rapes, Medina says, each one just as brutal. And

now, one drunken night of violence may have landed him a death sentence. Medina fears he has contracted the AIDS virus from his attackers… "Do you know how hard it is to see this happening to your son," asked Shawn's father, Luis Medina, a glassmaker. "What my son did was wrong, but no one on the planet deserves this."[31]

The Globe article continued:

"What I did was stupid…It was wrong," Medina says. "But nowhere in the book of rules was it written that I got here to get raped, that I have to have them destroy my mind, that I am supposed to get AIDS. That wasn't supposed to be the deal." After three rapes – or being "turned out," as the victims of rape are referred to in prison – Medina has given in to a kind of sexual slavery. He exchanges sex for survival, he says.[32]

Likewise, *The Chicago Sun-Times* (among many other newspapers) related the story of Illinois prison rape victim, Michael Eric Blucker, reportedly the first documented case in which a prisoner converted from HIV-negative to seropositive while in custody:

A male prisoner sued state prison officials in federal court Monday, charging that they violated his civil rights by ignoring his pleas for help against inmate rapes, which gave him the virus that causes AIDS…Blucker was sentenced in 1993 to 10 years on a theft conviction, said his mother, Sue Blucker. "You expect your son will someday come out of prison and get his life together. You don't expect him to be raped and come out of prison with AIDS," she said…State Rep. Cal Skinner Jr. (R-Crystal Lake) called the situation faced by Blucker and other inmates "an unadjudicated death sentence" said an unpublished study by the federal Centers for Disease Control and Prevention estimates that 100 Illinois prisoners per year contract HIV while incarcerated – 5000 nationally.[33]

Similarly, The Richmond Times-Dispatch offered the following example:

It was 1996. DeBlasio, who later served time in a Virginia prison, had been convicted of interstate trafficking of forged securities. He knew Milan was a tough place, but at 6 feet, 2 inches tall and 210 pounds, he didn't think he'd be sexually assaulted. He was wrong. He was raped more than 30 times over two months by the knife-wielding gang leader who was backed up by gang members. DeBlasio's attacker was a violent, emotionally disturbed, repeat offender. And he also had AIDS. DeBlasio became HIV-positive. He said he had always followed safe-sex practices previously and was sure he got infected in prison.[34]

Finally, *The Arkansas Democrat-Gazette* provides the example of prisoner, Kendell Spruce:

ADC [Arkansas Department of Corrections] is just like a big old family. Even convicts are part of the family," Norris [ADC Director] said at the conference, which brought together state and federal officials to discuss the Prison Rape Elimination Act…Kendell Spruce didn't feel like a part of the Correction Department's family. The Arkadelphia native went to prison for the first time in the early 1990s on a forgery conviction. He was 28. Within days, he said, he was sexually assaulted. By the time he left the Cummins Unit in early 1992, he said, 27 different men had sexually assaulted him hundreds of times. He said inmates paid guards in cigarettes, candy, and soda to "turn a deaf ear" to his cries for help. "It was regular, hourly. Oh lord, I was dead. I was tossed aside, and here comes another one," said Spruce, now 42 and living outside Flint, Mich. I saw guys getting stabbed, beat up, killed. I didn't want that to happen to me." Said Spruce, who claims he contracted HIV, the virus that causes AIDS, from his attackers.[35]

Reports on the plight of individual rape victims were commonly supported by statistics that aimed to quantify the magnitude of the "epidemic" problem of prison rape for newspaper readers. For example, *The Boston Globe* reported:

Across the country, it is estimated that every year, 200,000 to 300,000 male inmates are sexually assaulted in prisons, jails, and juvenile detention centers. Based on studies that show about 15 percent of males in state prisons are the victims of sexual assaults, there could be as many as 1,500 men every year raped behind bars in Massachusetts.[36]

In 2002, *The Washington Post* referred to prison rape as "a scourge that is estimated to affect some 175,000 Americans annually, Normally fodder for stand-up comics, prison rape is in fact one of the principal untreated human rights abuses in America today."[37] Likewise, the Associated Press reported in 2003 that "more than one in 10 inmates is believed to be raped while in prison";[38] the South Bend Tribune noted "No conclusive national data exists regarding the prevalence of this phenomenon, but the most recent statistical survey, published in the Prison Journal revealed that 21 percent of inmates in seven Midwestern prisons had experienced at least one episode of forced sex since being incarcerated";[39] and *The Birmingham News* stated, "Studies estimate between 22 and 25 percent of prisoners in state and federal facilities are victims of sexual assault or rape. On average, 10 percent of state prisoners will be raped, according to one estimate."[40] In 2004, the Associated Press reported, "sexual assaults occur...They're much more predominant than what you see in the statistics."[41]

As previously discussed, throughout the 1990s, various religious and human rights organizations, including Stop Prisoner Rape, Human Rights Watch, and Prison Fellowship Ministries, along with a number of human rights organizations working under the auspices of the United Nations, focused their energies on rendering prison rape visible on the national radar and constituting the issue as a critical social problem warranting immediate legislative action at both state and national levels. Likely reflecting the success of these organizations and others, after the turn of the century articles that deployed a human rights script increasingly contained calls for legislation aimed at eliminating prison rape in U.S. carceral facilities. Thus, the plethora of articles reporting on events leading up to and following passage of the Prison Rape Elimination Act of 2003 commonly employed a discourse of human rights in constructing prison rape for the news-reading public. A 2001 article in *The Houston Chronicle*, for example, reported, "A coalition of religious and human rights groups, horrified by the widespread rape of men in U.S. prisons and the public's apparent lack of concern, is pressing for a federal law to make state prison authorities accountable for sexual abuse of prisoners by prisoners."[42] The Richmond, Virginia *Times Dispatch* noted that proposed legislation to address the problem of prison rape "is not a liberal or conservative issue...It's an issue of basic decency and human rights."[43] Likewise, articles in *The Washington Post* and the *Birmingham News* provide examples of the blending of human rights discourse and calls for legislative intervention to address the problem of prison rape. In "Reform Plan Targets Prison Rape," Washington's *Post* noted:

> Rapes in the American prison system, for decades considered a sordid fact of life, will be analyzed and targeted for prevention under a new government program that marks a sea change in the awareness of sexual assaults by and against incarcerated men...Congressional sponsors ranged from Sen. Edward M. Kennedy (D-Mass.) to Sen. Jeff Sessions (R-Ala.), and supporting agencies ranges from the Christian Coalition to the NAACP...."Everyone has basic human rights, even if they are being dealt with and sanctioned for inappropriate social behavior, and prison should not take those away."[44]

Similarly, the *Birmingham News* reported on efforts to pass prison rape legislation in Washington:

> Sen. Jeff Sessions, who once had a career sending people to prison, on Thursday announced legislation to tackle the apparently prevalent but not-well-documented problem of sexual assaults behind bars. "They're still children of God," Sessions said...."It's not moral, it's not just, it's wrong...and it can leave bad emotional scars."...Chuck Colson, Chairman of Prison Fellowship Ministries, said rape has been an issue in all 600 prisons he has visited over the years. "Everybody knows it goes on but nobody wants to talk about it," Colson said.[45]

Crime

Framing prison rape in a discourse about rights was by no means the only construction employed in contemporary-era print news media. Indeed, after 1991, an increasing number of articles published in U.S. newspapers framed sexual violence in prisons as a crime. More than 25% of the articles published during the contemporary period framed prison rape as a criminal offense. Articles that employed this frame generally relied on one of two scripts, either representing correctional officers as accused perpetrators/defendants in criminal proceedings related to prison rape or casting prisoners in that role.

The Crime of Officer Sexual Misconduct

As stated in the introduction to this chapter, although staff-on-inmate sexual misconduct was neither illegal nor criminal in most jurisdictions until the latter decades of the twentieth century, during this period – specifically during the first half of the 1990s – federal and state legislative actions increasingly led to the criminalization of officer sexual misconduct in many jurisdictions. By 1996, the U.S. Congress and more than half of U.S. state legislatures had passed laws that defined sexual misconduct by correctional staff as a criminal offense and these legal changes were not overlooked by the press. During late 1990s and the early years following the turn of the century, report after report appeared in U.S. newspapers – articles that described the arrest and trial of correctional officers on charges of rape and sexual assault of prisoners. During this period the news-reading public was exposed to scores of titles like "Jailer Charged with Inmate Rape,"[46] "Guard at Juvenile Detention Center Arrested,"[47] "Nab Guard on Inmate Rape Charge,"[48] "Former Guard Jailed in Teen Inmate's Rape,"[49] and "Fired Corrections Officer Bound Over for Trial on Rape Charge."[50] Indeed, of the 78 contemporary-era articles that framed prison rape as a crime, 83.3% (65 articles) deployed a script that represented a current or former correctional employee as the accused perpetrator of prison rape. It should also be noted that, of the 65 articles framing prison rape as a crime and deploying a "sexual misconduct" script, 96.9% (63 articles) involved the rape or sexual assault of a female inmate by a correctional officer. In general, articles pertaining to the rape of male inmates framed the subject primarily as a rights-related issue, not as a crime.

The law has long defined rape and other forms of sexual assault as crimes, regardless of the venue in which they occur. Until recently, however, the circumstances surrounding rape and sexual assault of prisoners by correctional officers had rendered the successful prosecution of these offenses in the criminal courts particularly problematic. A series of articles published in 1992 highlight the legal dilemmas associated with prosecuting correctional officers for the sexual victimization of prisoners in the years prior to criminalization of officer-on-prisoner sexual misconduct. Appearing in the *Lewiston Morning Tribune* (Lewiston, Idaho), these articles related events surrounding the alleged 1991 rape of a female inmate at the Idaho Correctional Institution-Orofino and the ensuing legal arguments surrounding the decision to arraign a male corrections officer on a charge of rape. The first article, published on March 21, 1992, was quite brief, succinctly reporting that the alleged rape of a female inmate was under investigation. "We've still got some steps we're going through, gathering evidence," the article quoted the local sheriff as saying. The officer alleged to have committed the offense has been suspended with pay," the article reported. [51]

A second article in the series reported that "Stephen D. Daniel, 39," the correctional officer alleged to have perpetrated the assaults, "was being held in Clearwater County Jail pending posting of a $5000 bond. A preliminary hearing on two counts of rape and one count of the infamous crime against nature (oral sex) has been scheduled for May 26."[52] Daniel's arrest followed more than a year-long investigation by the local sheriff's department that included:

> state-of-the-art forensic DNA analysis of physical evidence in addition to accusations made by two alleged victims.[T]he delay in filing charges revolved around inadequacies in Idaho's rape statute....While refusing to discuss any of the specifics of the case, Clearwater County Prosecutor John A. Swayne said, "The state needs a law that prohibits any kind of sex between inmates and prison staff." But Idaho has no such statute and the case will therefore have to be prosecuted as any other rape case; whereby the state must prove that the sexual act was without consent. Three separate incidents are alleged in the criminal complaint. Count one alleges that Daniel, on or about March 8 or 9, 1991, "did physically and by his

position as a prison guard overcome thee resistance of a female inmate and had sexual intercourse."[53]

The final article in the series showcased the problems involved in prosecuting Daniel in the absence of a statute criminalizing all staff-on-inmate sexual misconduct.

Although a decision had been made to prosecute the officer for "the crime against nature" (oral sex)], an offense that could be considered a crime whether or not force was involved in its perpetration, as the article reported:

> Magistrate Patrick D. Costello of Orofino took under advisement Wednesday night whether Daniel should be bound over to the higher court on a charge of rape. His decision is expected sometime today. Critical to Costello's ruling is his interpretation of how much and what kind of resistance an alleged victim must exert under Idaho's rape statute. "Her lack of resistance is totally understandable," Costello said, referring to former inmate Margaret Marks, now of Boise. Marks testified last week that she was subjected to months of sexual abuse by Daniel while she was an inmate at the Idaho Correctional Institution-Orfino. But while Costello said he was convinced the alleged sexual intercourse was "non-consensual" on the part of Marks, he seemed to heed defense attorney Paul Thomas Clark's contention that, under Idaho law, physical resistance must be shown to prove rape...Marks, in her testimony, admitted she did not resist Daniel physically when he had intercourse with her. Instead she said she went into a "fog" as he took advantage of his power over her as a correctional officer. Clearwater County Prosecutor John A. Swayne conceded the rape count against Daniel begs for something other than a "traditional interpretation of Idaho's rape law. He suggested that Daniel, through his position of authority, held a "psychic compelling force" over Marks that made it impossible for her to show traditional physical resistance. Her non-participation in the acts, Swayne said, was virtually all the resistance Marks could muster under the circumstances.[54]

Some years later, in 1999, the Cleveland, Ohio *Plain Dealer* and the *Lewiston Morning Tribune* reported on state and federal-level concerns about officer-on-inmate sexual misconduct, this time in light of the rapidly growing population of female inmates in U.S. jails and prisons and the legal changes in the treatment of officer-on-inmate sexual misconduct that had begun to emerge in the early 1990s. On March 13, 1999, the *Lewiston Morning Tribune* remarked on the fact that Washington had just become the 39th state in the union to criminalize sex between guards and inmates. The *Morning Tribune* noted:

> When you're in prison and the guard watching you has the keys to your cell, weapons at his disposal and the ability to make your life tolerable or a living hell, it gets pretty tough to tell when sex with him is truly consensual. Just because you don't dare resist or rep[ort him to his superiors doesn't mean you consented...Consensual sex in situations where one party has total, potentially violent control over another and the other can't get away is the kind of consensual sex that takes place between 30-year-olds and 14-year-olds – a violation even with consent. At best it is shooting fish in a barrel. At worst it is savage, a type of police brutality. And the surest way to put a lid on it is to make consent legally impossible.[55]

The Cleveland, Ohio *Plain Dealer* noted the efforts of women in Congress to address or reinforce at a federal level the issue of "improper sexual contact"[56] between female prisoners and guards that at least 38 states had already addressed at a legislative level:

> "Corrections officers around the country have a tough job to do under difficult circumstances and we're not indicting them," said Cleveland Democratic Rep. Stephanie Tubbs Jones. "But those who do violate the law, we're not going to allow it, and we'll do all we can to make the necessary changes." Tubbs Jones said the House Judiciary Committee should pass a pending bill that would require better records on sexual misconduct with inmates, and require that states specifically train personnel to avoid it and pass laws against it to qualify for funding. Ohio Bureau of Prisons spokesman Joe

Andrews said any sexual contact between corrections officers and inmates is already illegal in Ohio, and state officer training programs stress the topic.[57]

In the context of ongoing efforts to criminalize staff-on-prisoner sexual misconduct in jurisdictions around the country, newspapers increasingly took note of the growing number of criminal trials related to sexual assaults by correctional officers and the circumstances that preceded events in the courtroom. A series of articles published in 1998 and 1999 in the Manchester, New Hampshire *Union Leader* exemplify articles that focused on the prosecution of correctional officers for sex crimes perpetrated against prisoners.   Published on September 29, 1998, the first article reported, "Belmont Rotary Club president Martin Mullen, 33, went on trial in Hillsborough County Superior Court, northern district, yesterday on a charge of raping a female inmate while he was working as a correctional officer at the New Hampshire State Prison for Women in Goffstown."[58] The prosecutor in the case against Mullen asserted that the alleged assault "was not about sex, it was about the 'misuse of power…about that man using his power to humiliate an inmate."[59]

On October 2, 1998, another article appeared in Manchester's *Union Leader*, this time stating, "Correctional Officer Mark Mullen was convicted yesterday on the charge of raping an inmate he was guarding in the New Hampshire State Prison for Women in Goffstown."[60] The article further noted:

The [victim] was serving a 30-day sentence for second-offense drunk driving when the attack took place, on April 30, 1996, just a few days before she was to be released. She had testified that during the humiliating assault, Mullen told her to shut up and not to bother reporting it because "no one would believe a drunk over an officer." Judge Carol Ann Conboy, who presided over the trial, revoked Mullen's bail, and Mullen, who is president of the Belmont Rotary Club, was escorted in handcuffs from the courtroom. Family members gathered outside, stunned and some in tears.[61]

Early the following year, on February 11, 1999, the Mullen case again garnered attention in the *Union Leader* when the former correctional officer was sentenced following his conviction on three felony counts, two of aggravated felonious sexual assault and one count of attempted aggravated felonious sexual assault. "Former Goffstown Women's Prison guard Martin Mullen, 33, yesterday was sentenced to 10 to 20 years in prison for raping a female inmate," the article reported.[62] Further, the *Union Leader* noted:

> It is important to be very clear about what happened between guard and inmate. "Mr. Mullen twice raped (the victim)....such an abuse of power and authority makes this crime especially egregious," [Judge Conboy] said. Conboy said the victim was under the absolute power of Mullen as a corrections officer, which should have offered her protection. He scarred the reputations of the honorable men and women in corrections work," she said.[63]

The Crime of Prisoner-on-Prisoner Rape

Incidents of prison rape that have resulted in the prosecution of inmate/perpetrators in the criminal courts have been, and remain, relatively rare occurrences. More often, incidents of prisoner-on-prisoner sexual violence that have not been ignored have been addressed "in-house" – that is, within the correctional system and out of sight of the press and general public. Accordingly, of the news articles that framed prison rape as a crime, relatively few cast prisoners as defendants in related criminal proceedings.

The following examples highlight the rarity of with which such a script was deployed in the contemporary-era print news media. First, in 1995, *The Boston Globe* reported on "what is being hailed as the first-ever criminal prosecution of a case of prison rape in Massachusetts."[64] *The Globe* noted:

> [L]aw enforcement officials have indicted an alleged accomplice in the sexual assault of a male inmate at the state prison in Concord. Harold Vilburn, 22, a former inmate at MCI-Concord now being held at Billerica House of Correction, is scheduled to be arraigned tomorrow in Middlesex Superior Court on charges of rape and conspiracy for acting as the "lookout" in the violent sexual assault last

year on a male inmate....Jerome Tibbs, 22, was charged last September with raping the alleged victim, a 26-year-old Fall River man.[65]

More than ten years after *The Boston Globe* article, in November 2006, *The Seattle Times* described a case of prison rape that occurred in Snohomish County, Washington. Noted by *The Times* as "the first such prosecution since the state enacted a new federal policy aimed at reducing prison rape," the case involved Washington prisoner Tremayne Francis, "a cellmate's worst nightmare."[66] Francis, convicted of raping two men while working as a martial-arts instructor in Pierce County, Washington, was serving a nine-year sentence at the Monroe Correctional Complex in Washington:

> [b]ut even behind razor wire, Francis used extortion and violence to force fellow inmates to have sex with him and raped two men new to prison, according to prison records. When confronted by prison staff, Francis, 34, claimed he had multiple-personality disorder and denied the rapes, claiming the sex was consensual, records show. Though found guilty of both rapes in prison hearings, the worst punishment he endured was solitary confinement and victim-awareness classes each time ending up back in the general prison population. But Francis is facing a criminal trial this week in Snohomish County Superior Court for the 2005 rape of an inmate at the Monroe Correctional Complex....Because of how unusual it is for prison rapes to become the focus of a criminal prosecution, the case has drawn the attention of the state Department of Corrections, as well as prosecutors and inmate-rights groups nationwide.[67]

Lies and Exaggeration

As was the case in the earlier time period, after 1992 news articles pertaining to prison rape periodically provided a forum for voices that cast doubt on the veracity and magnitude of the problem of prison rape. As was also the case prior to the contemporary period, these voices came primarily from, or represented the interests of, corrections. One of the most widely heard was that of Reginald Wilkinson, head of the

Ohio Department of Rehabilitation and Correction and former head of the American Correctional Association. In a December 26, 2002 letter to the *Cincinnati Enquirer* in which he criticized calls for legislative intervention to address the problem of prison rape, Wilkinson asserted, "Correctional jurisdictions don't need this law to prove what we already know; sexual assault in prison is highly exaggerated."[68] Wilkinson further contended that prison rape is widespread is "a flat-out lie."

Far from marginal in corrections, Wilkinson's voice was joined by a number of others in the industry contending that allegations of widespread rape were either not applicable in their particular jurisdiction or that such allegations were outrageous exaggerations. Unnamed correctional officials in Utah, for example, claimed that "inmate advocacy groups are inflating rape statistics, and point[ed] to the low number of rape reports as proof."[69] Similarly, in 2001, the South Carolina Department of Corrections noted in the Rock Hill, South Carolina *Herald* that only two rapes had been reported in the entire history of the State's prison system.[70]

Articles reporting on failed attempts by prisoners to sue for civil rights violations should not be overlooked in terms of their contribution to the counter-discourse casting doubt on the veracity of prison rape allegations. The case of Michael E. Blucker, who accused Illinois State prison employees of neglecting to help him when he was allegedly raped and sold as a "sex slave," provides an example. A widely distributed Copley News Service article reporting on the outcome of Blucker's suit noted:

> Katherine Novak, legal counsel for the Illinois Department of Corrections, said Blucker was after money when he sued state employees. Corrections officials believe Blucker contracted HIV either outside the prison system or by having consensual sex, she said. "I think there was testimony from some of our witnesses about Mr. Blucker engaging in consensual sex and about having a drug habit," Novak said. "He's a three-time offender. I think this was about money."[71]

Just Deserts

The notion that the role of corrections is to insure that lawbreakers receive exactly the measure of punishment they are due, nothing more and nothing less has dominated the discourse about criminal justice throughout the contemporary era. This "just deserts" model holds that every criminal activity entails a specific measure of punishment and the distribution of that punishment is the only responsibility of the criminal justice system in its relationship with criminals. Interestingly, in the early years of the contemporary period, a number of articles published in U.S. newspapers framed prison rape as a part of the punishment that at least some lawbreakers rightly deserve. Indeed, a series of letters published between August 1995 and February 1996 in the widely syndicated "Ann Landers" column illuminated the breadth of Americans' opinions about the extent of the measure of punishment criminals deserve and, indeed, the depth of the sentiment associated with those opinions.

On August 9, 1995, a letter appeared in Landers' column from "Outraged in Michigan." "Outraged" expressed concern about the epidemic of rape plaguing the U.S. prison system after seeing a documentary film on the subject. "I've never heard an outcry from any human rights group on this subject," "Outraged wrote, "and I have never heard my church speak about it. This is a hideous problem – and it's real. We really ought to give a damn."[72]

Three letters in response to "Outraged" are noteworthy in that they express points of view that may be widely held but, at the same time, are rarely aired in the press. On October 22, 1995, the first, from "Also Outraged," appeared in "Ann Landers." The letter began:

> This is for the person in Michigan who whined about prison rape in a recent column. I'm sick and tired of thugs behind bars bellyaching and going on strike because they don't like the food. I wish the millions spent for health and dental care and recreation for jailbirds could be diverted to help the homeless. Most prisoners have better food and medical attention than the average working stiff who obeys the law and plays by the rules. While I don't condone physical abuse under any circumstances, the solution to the problem is simple –

don't do the crime and you won't have to worry about doing
the time.[73]

The next letter, from a writer who signed him/herself "P.O.'D,"
echoed the basic sentiment expressed by "Also Outraged," but in
somewhat more rancorous terms:

> Dear Ann Landers: Most people think prisoners are treated
> too well. I agree. Our justice system stinks. Recently, a man
> was on trial for murdering his girlfriend. She worked in a mall
> here in Louisville. As she entered her car to go home, he shot
> her several times. He had raped her two weeks earlier and was
> out on bail. His sentence was announced yesterday. He got
> life, which is 12 years here in Kentucky, which means he'll
> probably be out in six or eight years. This is outrageous. If he
> gets raped in prison, I couldn't care less.[74]

Finally, on October 30, 1995, "M. in Fla." wrote:

> My daughter, age 23, was brutally raped and murdered. The
> death certificate read "Skull crushed by blunt object. Multiple
> stab wounds on the neck and body." The murderer finally
> confessed, so that animal who raped and killed my daughter is
> now living rent-free, getting three square meals a day and free
> dental and medical care, watching cable TV, exercising in a
> gym and working on a master's degree – thanks to the
> generosity of us taxpayers. When I read letters about
> protecting criminals from "cruel and inhuman treatment," my
> blood boils. How many of those animals thought about the
> cruel and inhuman treatment of their victims? I have zero
> sympathy for them.[75]

While the sentiments expressed in the latter three letters by no
means represent a dominant discourse in the press during this or any
other time period, it would be a mistake to discount them as marginal.
Indeed, even today similar opinions are regularly expressed in the
context of message boards and other web-based forums, as well as in
day-to-day talk among individuals and in the discourse generated by
certain groups. Further, the sentiments revealed in the Landers letters

may also be understood as underpinning remarks such as those made by former California Attorney General Bill Lockyer, who said at a press conference about Enron Corporation Chairman Kenneth Lay, "I would love to personally escort Lay to an 8-by-10 cell that he could share with a tattooed dude who says, 'Hi, my name is Spike, honey.'"[76]

ASSIGNING BLAME

Shifting Attributions

Prior to 1992, articles published in U.S. newspapers had overwhelmingly framed carceral rape as a symptom of institutional failure, depicting the problem as a signal that prisons were out of control and failing along various critical dimensions of correctional performance. Accordingly, much of the blame for the problem of prison rape was attributed to a failed or failing correctional system, as well as to the particularly problematic "types" of prisoners it housed and attempted to control. In contrast, in the era of "just deserts," the representation of corrections as a failing institution no longer dominated the discourse. Indeed, the press's earlier penchant for framing prison rape as a symptom of correctional failure declined and eventually all but disappeared from the discourse generated by the print news media in the contemporary era. In its place, prison rape came to be framed in a number of new ways – predominantly as a rights issue and as a criminal offense. Accordingly, in assigning blame for the problem, articles that employed these new frames largely abandoned the scripts that had been deployed in the earlier time period and began to draw on others with increasing frequency.

Articles published in the contemporary period all but ceased to cast the "homosexual" in the role of prison rapist. By this time, homosexuals had been recast as weak, inagentive individuals – the quintessential *victims* of rape rather than fearsome perpetrators. Indeed, as was the case toward the end of the preceding time period, in the contemporary era a number of the articles published made it clear that prison rapists were to be understood as heterosexual, not homosexual, and that prison rape was to be understood as an act of power and not as an expression of sexuality. Accordingly, none of the contemporary era articles in the data set identified homosexuals as perpetrators of prison rape.

Only a handful of articles published during this period overtly pointed the finger of blame for prison rape at African-American or other "non-white" prisoners. At the same time, the press deployed a number of "signals" that communicated perpetrators' non-white race (e.g. names typical of African-American culture, gang affiliations, physical descriptions of perpetrators that intimated race) without specifically identifying perpetrators as not "white."[77] Additionally, by the beginning of the contemporary era, the specter of the hyper-sexual, violent black male was firmly entrenched in the popular imagination and the notion that "most" prisoners – in particular those of a violent and recalcitrant nature – were African-American had become almost axiomatic in the culture.[78] Thus, identification of rapists' race may have seemed unnecessary or redundant to some journalists and readers.

On the whole, the tendency to deploy scripts blaming specific "types" of prisoners for the problem of carceral rape declined in the press during the contemporary era. As noted earlier, by this time, "homosexuals" and "homosexuality" had ceased to be blamed for the problem altogether. Further, while they were identified – overtly or subtly – as perpetrators, African-Americans and other non-whites did not bear the brunt of the blame for prison rape writ large – that is prison rape constituted as a pervasive social problem in the contemporary era. Instead, after 1992, articles published in elite and popular newspapers overwhelmingly placed the weight of blame for the problem on the pernicious institutional culture of corrections, on rogue correctional officers, and, less often, at the doorstep of an apathetic public that failed to take an interest in the plight of its cast-off "social junk."

Blaming Institutional Culture

By 1992, the print news media had all but ceased to depict corrections as a dysfunctional or failing institution. Although specific issues like overcrowding, understaffing, a pervasive culture of violence, and a lack of adequate funding were identified in the press as ongoing issues that plagued the industry and contributed to the incidence of sexual assaults in U.S. prisons, references to correctional deterioration, dysfunction, disarray and failure were far less frequent in the contemporary press than they had been in the historical era. If the contemporary era press held corrections at fault for the problem of prison rape at all – and it did – it was not because the system was either failing or hopelessly dysfunctional. Instead, the press pointed to a new source of blame – a pernicious correctional culture that ignored, tolerated, facilitated, and sometimes encouraged rape and other forms of sexual violence in American carceral facilities. As *The Columbian*, a Vancouver, Washington newspaper noted in 1994:

> Perhaps the most problematic aspect of prisoner rape is the tacit acquiescence of corrections officials. It's one thing for some violent male criminals, locked away for years, to attempt rape as a vehicle for social domination, sexual release or both. It's quite another for law enforcement personnel to wink at the problem. Prison authorities generally deny that rape exists in their institutions and take few steps to prevent it.[79]

As the article suggests, by the 1990s sexual violence committed by one inmate on another – while not acceptable – had become somewhat understandable to the press. It was correctional officials' tolerance of sexual violence that was increasingly understood as glaringly problematic – and blameworthy. Of the total articles published during this time period, more than 30% deployed a script attributing blame for prison rape to corrections' problematic institutional culture. Corrections' tolerance of prison rape was highlighted in an October 2005 article by the Associated Press State & Local Wire which noted in regard to the alleged rape of Texas inmate, Roderick Johnson:

> The truth is that until now, rape has been "a part of the penalty" paid by criminal offenders. Rape of men by men has been a penalty administered by the prisoner power structure. Worse, it's been the penalty ignored or tacitly accepted by many of those who call themselves corrections officials.[80]

Johnson claimed to have been raped and sold as a sex slave by gangs during his 18 months at the Allred Unit near Wichita Falls, Texas, "while callous prison officials never investigated his reports of abuse or kept him in a safer area for vulnerable inmates," the article claimed. "[Johnson] said some employees made fun of him during committee hearings and told him to fight the other inmates or get a boyfriend for protection."[81] In another Associated Press article related to the Johnson case, it was noted that:

Prison officials were well aware of his plight, but refused to conduct any meaningful investigation of his complaints and refused his repeated pleas to be housed in safekeeping," 'Prison officials knew that gangs made Roderick Johnson their sex slave and did nothing to help him,' said Margaret Winter, associate director of the ACLU's National Prison Project....they threw out client to the wolves." The suit also said officials at the Allred Unit "failed to take reasonable measures to prevent him from being victimized" by numerous prison gangs."[82]

Like the widely publicized case of Roderick Johnson in Texas, the alleged rape of Michael Blucker in a Massachusetts prison (discussed earlier in this chapter) received extensive press coverage. In the context of more than a few articles reporting on Blucker's case, it was alleged that the victim had "complained to numerous prison employees that he was being raped and forced to smuggle drugs into the maximum-security prison, but that no one rescued him from the situation." "In this culture, a man who complains to officials is told, 'Toughen up punk,'" the article related. The facts of Blucker's case "produced more shrugs of acceptance than cries of outrage," the article continued. "Asked about the assaulted prisoner who may have contracted HIV, a Massachusetts Department of Corrections spokesman echoed the sentiment perfectly. 'Well,' he said, 'that's prison. Boys will be boys, prisoners will be prisoners.'"[83]

Blaming "Rogue" Officers

In addition to blaming the culture of corrections for the problem of prison rape, a large number of articles published in the contemporary era deployed a script that blamed at least part of the problem on "rogue officers," correctional officers and other staff who abused their position of power to arrange for or perpetrate acts of rape and other forms of sexual assault against prisoners placed in their charge. While at first glance this script and the "institutional culture" script may both seem to point a finger at corrections, the two are in fact distinct from one another. When the press deployed the institutional culture script, the blame for prison rape was indeed placed at the door of corrections. In contrast, the "rogue officer" was depicted as acting on his own – well outside the boundaries of correctional culture. In a nutshell, rogue officers were represented as "bad apples" – aberrant, sometimes criminal officers (or groups of officers) who betrayed the public trust as well as the trust of the industry that had employed them. Thus, the actions of rogue officers did not directly implicate corrections but focused blame on specific aberrant individuals employed, or far more often *previously* employed, in the industry.

Among the articles published during the contemporary period, about 34% deployed a script attributing blame for the problem of prison rape to rogue officers. Not surprisingly, articles that framed prison rape primarily as a crime were most likely to blame rogue officers, while opinions that framed it as a principally as a rights issue drew on that script far less often. Interestingly, articles representing prison rape as a *constitutional rights* issue were more apt to deploy the rogue officer script than were those that depicted the problem primarily as a *human rights* issue.

Articles that relied on the rogue officer script commonly bore titles like "Former Jailer Indicted on Rape Charge,"[84] "Former Guard Convicted of Raping Inmate,"[85] "Turley Ex-Guard Found Guilty in Inmate Rape,"[86] "Ex-Guard Convicted of Raping Inmate Gets 12 ½ Years Behind Bars."[87] The depictions of the perpetrators as "Ex-" or "Former" guards seem to effectively separate these individuals from the correctional system that had employed them. Correctional officers who perpetrated sexual assaults were depicted as "bad apples." Further, articles that blamed rogue officers for prison rape depicted these individuals in terms that rendered them more like "criminals" than like correctional personnel. Rogue officers, for example, were frequently described as "accused,"[88] "arrested,"[89] "in handcuffs,"[90] "indicted,"[91] "escorted from the courtroom," "found guilty,"[92] "convicted,"[93] and "sentenced to prison for the rape of a female inmate."[94]

Many of these articles offered comments from correctional administrators that reveal official disappointment and sometimes disgust over the actions of these individuals and, at the same time, served to further establish distance between officer/perpetrators and the institutions that provided the venue for their crimes. A report published on December 16th, 2005 in the Little Rock *Arkansas Democrat-Gazette* is representative of this discourse:

"Our stance is that no inmate can consent," said Dina Tyler,
spokesman for the Corrections Department. "We do not
believe an actual rape has occurred but there's no excuse for
this. You are trained since the day you take this job not to
have sex with inmates."..."It concerns me that we have staff
that choose to engage in behavior like this. It is frustrating to
me as an administrator," Warden Grant Harris said.[95]

In the case of former Goffstown Women's Prison guard, Martin
Mullen (discussed previously), who was convicted of raping a teenage
inmate in New Hampshire, the Manchester *Union Leader* reported,
"Mullen was given a badge, a uniform, and authority but he misused
it,"[96] and, in another article noted that Mullen's "abuse of power and
authority makes his crime especially egregious...He scarred the
reputations of the honorable men and women in corrections work."[97]
Similarly, an article distributed by the Associated Press reported on the
rape conviction of a former Texas prison guard: "Miller's abhorrent
behavior is inexcusable, and is certainly not representative of the fine
folks at the Bureau of Prisons who are highly motivated, professional
employees."[98]   Likewise, the St. Petersburg Times reported on the
guilty verdict in the case a Florida officer charged with rape, stating,
"'It's clear from the evidence that he abused the state's trust. We take
these matters extremely seriously and we have zero tolerance for abuse
of state prisoners by state employees.'"[99]

Blaming the Public

The notion that the public should bear some of the blame for problem
of prison rape was not entirely unvoiced in the contemporary era press
but, as was the case in the historic period, it remained a relatively minor
discourse. Indeed, the number of articles published annually that
blamed the public for prison rape remained relatively constant across
both the historical and the contemporary periods. Over time, however,
there were discernable qualitative changes in exactly how the public
was understood to share culpability for the problem of prison rape.
First, while half of the articles in the earlier period suggested that the
public's inaction was due to ignorance, this was not the case in the
contemporary era. Indeed, after 1992 few if any articles alleged that
the public was *unaware* that prison rape was occurring. Instead, the

contemporary press pointed an accusatory finger at the public's "overt and systemic indifference"[100] to prison rape and at an overarching retributive mood pervasive in the culture.

Referencing the suicide of prison rape victim, Rodney Hulin, a reporter for the *Pasadena Star-News* remarked on the public's callous indifference: "Hey, that's prison, you might say. Don't do the crime if you can't do the time...but this is about sexual torture of the helpless, aided and abetted by the indifference of prison officials and the wider society."[101]   "In this supposed civilized nation, prison rape is considered part of the punishment process....The public and comics openly snigger at the possibility of rape while someone is incarcerated," the Columbus, Ohio Post-Dispatch noted.[102]   Further, on July 23, 2003, *The Hill* called prison rape "a weird and serious problem that society has come to joke about. Part of the reason is that rage at criminals exploded during the 1990s."[103]   Finally, an article that appeared in the *Richmond Times Dispatch* noted with distaste the following comment from an unidentified member of the local public:

> Well, here we are treating adults like they're children and that's what bothers me. These are the same people that brought fear and nightmares into somebody's life. They come to prison after causing whatever mayhem they may have caused, and all of a sudden now we want to say: "Look at this poor person. You must make all the decisions for him and if you don't you're at fault. These are adults, adult men. They need...to protect themselves.[104]

Although articles attributing a portion of the blame for the problem of prison rape to public indifference amounted to a relatively minor discourse during the contemporary era, over time an increasing number of articles – in particular those representing prison rape as a human rights issue – seem to have been directed at and intended to generate concern among a culpably apathetic public. Particularly around the turn of the last century, as the discourse in the print media began to coalesce in favor of a legislative response to the problem, the voice of human rights in the press increasingly included a component that spoke of the need to mobilize an indifferent and apathetic American public.

[1] Lipton, Douglas, R. Martinson, and J. Wilks, *The Effectiveness of Correctional Treatment: A Survey of Treatment valuation Studies*, Praeger Press, New York.

[2] Howard, Lucy, Gerald C. Lubenow, and Stephan Lesher. "What Prisons Should Do." Newsweek. February 10, 1975: 36.

[3] "What Works? Questions and Answers about Prison Reform." *Public Interest* 10:22-54.

[4] Prison Litigation Reform Act of 1995, Pub. L. No. 104-134 (codified as amended in scattered titles and sections of the U.S.C.); *see also* H.R. 3019, 104th Cong. (1996).

[5] Ibid.

[6] *Integration of the Human Rights of Women and the Gender Perspective: Violence Against Women: Addendum.* Report of the Special Rapporteur on violence against women, its causes and consequences, Ms. Radhika Coomaraswamy, in accordance with Commission on Human Rights resolution 1997/44. Distr.GENERAL E/CN.4/1999/68/Add.2

[7] Ibid.

[8] "The Body: The Complete HIV/AIDS Resource: http://www.thebody.com/content/whatis/art12206.html. (last visited 5/10/08).

[9] "Poll Finds Wide Concern about Prison Rape." *The Boston Globe.* May 17, 1994.

[10] "The Double Punishment in American Prisons." *The Boston Globe.* June 12, 1994.

[11] "Court Hears Lawsuit from Transsexual in Prison Rape Case." *The Commercial Appeal*, Memphis, Tennessee. January 13, 1994.

[12] "Transsexual Inmate's Rape Suit Reinstated." *The Chicago Sun-Times.* June 7, 1994.

[13] "Court Sets Rules for Suit on Jail Rape." *The Boston Globe.* June 7, 1994.

[14] "Transsexual Inmate's Rape Suit Reinstated." *The Chicago Sun-Times.* June 7, 1994.

[15] "Former Lamb County Inmate Awarded $287,500 in 1999 Jail Rape." The Associated Press State & Local Wire: Dateline: Lubbock, Texas. February 20, 2000.

[16] "Federal Jury Awards $4 Million to Former Prisoner in Rape Case." The Associated Press State & Local Wire: Dateline: Fort Worth, Texas. June 3, 2003.

[17] "Former Inmate Files $6 Million Rape Lawsuit." *The Knoxville News-Sentinel.*" September 9, 1996.

[18] "Fisher Sues for $20 Million Over Alleged Prison Rape." *The Times Union*, Albany, New York. September 25, 1996.

[19] "State Settles Prison Rape Charge for $36,000." The Associated Press State & Local Wire: Dateline: Portland, Maine. October 14, 1998.

[20] "Settlement Expected Over Rape Allegation: Woman Says She Was Assaulted by Male Inmate Placed in Her County Jail Cell." *The St. Louis Post-Dispatch*. February 17, 2006.

[21] "Inmates Lawsuit Alleges St. Lucie Deputy Raped Her." *The Palm Beach Post*. December 30, 1995.

[22] "Appeals Court Orders New Trial on Damages in Prison Rape." *St Louis Post-Dispatch*. February 7, 1992.

[23] Ibid.

[24] "S.F. Agrees to Spend $4.5 Million on Jail: San Bruno Inmates' Suit Prompts Tentative Pact." *The San Francisco Chronicle*. March 8, 1993.

[25] "Lawsuit Brought Attention to Prison Rape." *The Chicago Daily Herald*. October 6, 1997.

[26] Ibid.

[27] Ibid.

[28] "No Award in Prison Rape Case!" *The St. Louis Post-Dispatch*. August 30, 1997.

[29] "Jury Vindicates Five Guards in Prison Rape Case." The Copley News Service. August 29, 1997.

[30] Jury Rejects Prison Rape Claim." The Associated Press State & Local Wire: Dateline: East St. Louis. August 29, 1997.

[31] "Prison's Hidden Horror: Rape Behind Bars." *The Boston Globe*. May 1, 1994.

[32] Ibid.

[33] "HIV-Positive Male Inmate Sues Prisons." *The Chicago Sun-Times*. April 25, 1995.

[34] "Prison-Rape Issue Gets Closer Look: Advocates Push Bill in Congress." *The Richmond Times-Dispatch*, Richmond, Virginia. July 10, 2003.

[35] "Federal Law Focuses on Sex Assaults in Prisons." *The Arkansas Democrat-Gazette*, Little Rock, Arkansas. June 9, 2005.

[36] "Officials Recoil at Culture of Rape in Prisons." *The Boston Globe*. May 4, 1994.

[37] "Prison Rape Is No Joke." *The Washington Post*. June 13, 2002.

[38] "Congress Nears Final Passage on Sessions' Measure to Curb Prison Rape." The Associated Press State & Local Wire. July 22, 2003.

[39] "Prison Rape Ignored." *South Bend Tribune*, South Bend Indiana. August 8, 2001.

[40] "Senators Target Rape in Prisons." *The Birmingham News*, Birmingham, Alabama. June 14, 2002.

[41] "Senate Stops Prison Rape Bill: House Could Revive." The Associated Press State & Local Wire. January 26, 2004.

[42] "Group Presses to Make Prisons Liable for Inmate Rapes." *The Houston Chronicle*. April 22, 2001.

[43] "Prison Rape Put in Spotlight: Group Calls for U.S. Standards." *Richmond Times Dispatch*, Richmond, Virginia. August 1, 2002.

[44] "Reform Plan Targets Prison Rape: Congress Unanimously Approves Study, Efforts to Stop Assaults." *The Washington Post*. July 26, 2003.

[45] "Senators Target Rape in Prisons." *The Birmingham News*, Birmingham, Alabama. June 14, 2002.

[46] "Jailer Charged with Inmate Rape." *Albuquerque Journal*, Albuquerque, New Mexico. June 28, 1998.

[47] "Guard at Juvenile Detention Center Arrested." The Associated Press State & Local Wire: Dateline: Santa Fe. April 3, 2003.

[48] "Nab Guard on Inmate Rape Charge." *New York Daily News*. January 30, 2002.

[49] "Former Guard Jailed in Teen Inmate's Rape." *Albuquerque Journal*, Albuquerque, New Mexico. April, 29, 2003.

[50] "Fired Corrections Officer Bound Over for Trial on Rape Charge." The Associated Press State & Local Wire. January 22, 2003.

[51] "Probe Continues in Alleged Prison Rape at Orofino." *Lewsiton Morning Tribune*, Lewiston Idaho. March 21, 1992.

[52] "Clearwater County Ex-Guard at Orofino Accused of Inmate Rapes." *Lewiston Morning Tribune*, Lewiston, Idaho. May 8, 1992.

[53] Ibid.

[54] "Sex in Prison Judge Weighs Prison Rape Charge Ruling Expected Today on Whether to Try Ex-Guard." *Lewiston Morning Tribune*, Lewiston, Idaho. July 9, 1992.

[55] "Even with "Consent' Sex with a Prison Guard is Rape." *Lewiston Morning Tribune*, Lewiston, Idaho. May 13, 1999.

[56] "Congresswomen Ask Halt to Female Prisoner Rapes." *The Plain Dealer*, Cleveland, Ohio. July 22, 1999.

[57] Ibid.

[58] "Guard's Trial Begins In Inmate Rape Case." *The Union Leader*, Manchester, New Hampshire. September 29, 1998.

[59] Ibid.

[60] "Correctional Officer Found Guilty of Inmate Rape." *The Union Leader*, Manchester, New Hampshire. October 2, 1998.

[61] Ibid.

[62] "Ex-Guard Gets 10 to 20 Years for Prison Rapes." *The Union Leader*, Manchester, New Hampshire. February 11, 1999.

[63] Ibid.

[64] "Prisoner Charged as Accomplice in Rape of MCI-Concord Inmate." *The Boston Globe*. February 13, 1995.

[65] Ibid.

[66] "Rare Criminal Trial Focuses Attention on 'Huge Problem' of Prison Rape." *The Seattle Times*. November 14, 2006.

[67] Ibid.

[68] "Federal Prison Rape Law Is Not Needed." *The Cincinnati Enquirer*. December 26, 2002.

[69] "Inmate Rape, Subject to Public Indifference, May Be Highlighted in Court Action." The Associated Press State & Local Wire. December 16, 2001.

[70] "Preventing Prison Rape." *The Herald*, Rock Hill, South Carolina. July 31, 2001.

[71] "Jury Vindicates Five Guards in Prison Rape Case." Copley News Service. August 29, 1997.

[72] "Risk of Prison Rape Exceeds Punishment That Inmates Deserve." *News & Record*, Greensboro, North Carolina. August 9, 1995.

[73] "Little Sympathy for Prison Rape Victims." *St. Louis Post-Dispatch*. October 22, 1995.

[74] Ibid.

[75] "Prisoners Don't Deserve Any Sympathy from Us." *The Ledger*, Lakeland, Florida. October 30, 1995.

[76] http://www.cato.org/pubs/papers/palmer-06-06-01.html   (last   visited: 05/18/2008)

[77] While initial coding for race revealed that only 3.7% of the articles specifically identified perpetrators as non-white, a second coding was undertaken which accounted for "signals" as well as statements of race. The second coding revealed that 10.1% (30 articles) of the articles published in the contemporary era identified perpetrators of prison rape as non-white (intercoder reliability = .78).

[78] See: Sloop, John M. (1996). *The Cultural Prison*. Tuscaloosa, Alabama: Univ. of Alabama Press.

[79] "Yes, Male Rape Does Happen." *The Columbian*, Vancouver, Washington. June 12, 1994.

[80] "Jurors Deliberating in Prison Rape Lawsuit." The Associated Press State and Local Wire: Dateline: Wichita Falls, Texas. October 18, 2005.

[81] Ibid.

[82] "Inmate Rape Claims Spawn Suit Against Texas Prison System." The Associated Press State and Local Wire: Dateline: Wichita Falls, Texas. April 18, 2002.

[83] "Jury Vindicates Five Prison Guards in Prison Rape Case." Copley News Service: Dateline: East St. Louis. August 29, 1997.

[84] "Former Jailer Convicted on Rape Charge." *Knoxville News-Sentinel*, Knoxville, Tennessee. March 1, 2002.

[85] "Former Guard Convicted." The Associated Press State & Local Wire: Dateline: Fort Worth, Texas. February 10, 2004.

[86] "Turley Ex-Guard Found Guilty in Inmate Rape." *Tulsa World*, Tulsa, Oklahoma. September 6, 2002.

[87] "Ex-Guard Convicted of Raping Inmate Gets 12 ½ Years Behind Bars." The Associated Press State & Local Wire: Dateline: Fort Worth, Texas. July 2, 2004.

[88] "Fired Prison Guard Pleads Guilty; Victim Says She Tried to Kill Herself." The Associated Press State & Local Wire: Dateline: Salt Lake City, Utah. May 13, 2003.

[89] Supermax Guard Admits to Sex Act with Inmate, Officials Say." *Arkansas Democrat-Gazette*, Little Rock, Arkansas. December 16, 2005.

[90] "Ex-Guard Gets 10 to 20 Years for Prison Rapes." *The Union Leader*, Manchester, New Hampshire. February 11, 1999.

[91] "Maui Jail Warden Indicted for Female Inmate Rape." The Associated Press State & Local Wire: Dateline: Honolulu, Hawaii. June 7, 2003.

[92] "Former Guard Found Guilty in Inmate's Rape." *St. Petersburg Times*, St. Petersburg, Florida. March 25, 1998.

[93] "Former Guard Convicted." The Associated Press State & Local Wire: Dateline: Fort Worth, Texas. February 10, 2004.

[94] "Ex-Guard Convicted of Raping Inmate Gets 12 ½ Years Behind Bars." The Associated Press State & Local Wire: Dateline: Fort Worth, Texas. July 2, 2004

[95] Supermax Guard Admits to Sex Act with Inmate, Officials Say." *Arkansas Democrat-Gazette*, Little Rock, Arkansas. December 16, 2005.

[96] Guard's Trial Begins in Inmate Rape Case." *The Union Leader*, Manchester, New Hampshire. September 29, 1998.

[97] "Ex-Guard Gets 10 to 20 Years for Prison Rapes." *The Union Leader*, Manchester, New Hampshire. February 11, 1999.

[98] "Ex-Guard Convicted of Raping Inmate Gets 12 ½ Years Behind Bars." The Associated Press State & Local Wire: Dateline: Fort Worth, Texas. July 2, 2004

[99] "Former Guard Found Guilty in Inmate's Rape." *St. Petersburg Times*, St. Petersburg, Florida. March 25, 1998.

[100] "Court Sets Rules for Suit on Jail Rape." *The Boston Globe*. June 7, 1994.

[101] "Bush Should Sign on Prison Rape Legislation." *Pasadena Star-News*, Pasadena, California. May 27, 2003.

[102] "Staff Members Are Not the Criminals in Prisons." *Columbus Dispatch*, Columbus, Ohio. April 20, 2003.

[103] "Liberals, Conservatives Jointly Target Prison Rape." *The Hill*, Washington, D.C. July 23, 2003.

[104] "Prisons Termed Ripe for Rapes." *Richmond Times Dispatch*, Richmond, Virginia. March 17, 1996.

CHAPTER FOUR

Prison Rape in the Courts, 1969-1991: The Historic Period

By the 1960s, the realization that the nation's prison system was failing to meet its objectives to protect the public, reduce crime, and rehabilitate offenders was firmly established in the public consciousness (Haas 1977). The rash of violence, riots, and escapes that swept through carceral facilities across the country during the preceding decade was widely interpreted as a signifier that the malignant and dysfunctional U.S. penal system was spiraling out of control. Increasing media exposure of the hellish world inside prison walls, coupled with almost daily reports of rising recidivism rates among released offenders, convinced many of the need for federal intervention to remedy the appalling conditions and widespread inadequacies of American corrections.

Mid-century legislators' and executive branch officials' disinclination to tackle the problems of American prisons led many interested parties to look to the courts as a potential source of relief (Haas 1977). Historically, however, the U.S. judiciary had maintained a hostile posture toward litigation relating to prison reform and the rights of incarcerated offenders. While the courts were the agency that delivered the convicted offender into incarceration, they traditionally had abandoned him/her at prison's gate. Indeed, once a prisoner passed into state custody, the courts were almost entirely unwilling to hear cases related to the conditions of his/her confinement. Instead, the judiciary maintained relatively strict adherence to a policy of non-intervention in prison affairs and almost universally declined jurisdiction in cases involving the rights of prisoners. In theory, this so-called "hands off doctrine"[1] did not preclude the courts from intervening in "exceptional circumstances" involving clear evidence of abuses that "degrade the individual and destroy the sense of personal honor."[2] In fact, they almost never did. Overwhelmingly, the judiciary subscribed to the notion that "[c]ourts are without power to supervise prison administration or to interfere with ordinary prison rules or regulations."[3]

Early manifestations of the hands-off doctrine were justified by alluding to the once commonly held view that the prisoner amounted to "a slave of the State," a status devoid of any enforceable rights.[4] By the early 20th century, however, the judiciary rarely expressed this position openly. Instead, later courts based their refusal to hear prison-related litigation on one or more of a number of rationales, including the theory of separation of powers; the notion that federalism precludes intervention on behalf of state prisoners; the lack of judicial expertise in the area of penology; the fear that judicial intervention would undermine prison discipline; and a belief that hearing *any* inmate complaints would open the floodgates to an overwhelming volume of similar cases (Haas 1977). In conjunction with the deployment of these rationales, the belief that the rights and protections afforded "law-abiding" citizens are forfeit at prison's gate likely remained an unvoiced motivation for judicial hostility to prisoner-generated litigation well into the modern era. Indeed, it was not until 1944, in *Coffin v. Reichard*,[5] that a panel of Sixth Circuit justices formally repudiated this idea and began to legally reconstitute the prisoner as an "incarcerated citizen" rather than a "slave of the State" (Feeley and Rubin 1999).

The early 1960s saw an expansion of the powers of the federal judiciary as actions brought through the civil rights movement and the tenor of the Warren Court expedited the move toward more active judicial intervention to define and protect individual rights. At the same time, the 1960s were producing broad challenges to social and economic policies in the form of vastly increased litigation coupled with protest activism (Berkman 1979). A significant change in the prison population began to occur during the mid-1960s as thousands of draft evaders entered federal prisons. Many of these prisoners were of middle-class background and, as a result, they were able to muster resources to attack policies they found repugnant. Blacks, by this time in the forefront of the struggle for social change in the community, brought their struggle into prisons. Along with these changes in the incarcerated population, changes were taking place in the legal community as well. In particular, a number of civil rights lawyers, experienced in litigation associated with earlier struggles, began to broaden their work to incorporate cases brought by members of the incarcerated population.

In conjunction with these various changes, the first half of the 1960s saw the hegemony of the hands-off doctrine begin to unravel as a number of court orders and decisions revealed heightened judicial scrutiny of conditions of confinement and broadened the circumstances under which prisoners could sue the system for their rights and other considerations. In 1962, for example, *Robinson v. State of California*[6] established that the Eighth Amendment ban on cruel and unusual punishment is applicable to the states as well as to the federal government. Shortly thereafter, in 1963, the court's decision in *Jones v. Cunningham*[7] gave inmates to ability to employ a writ of habeas corpus to challenge the conditions of their confinement as well as the legality of their sentencing.   The following year, the U.S. Supreme Court's ruling in *Cooper v. Pate* (1964)[8] gave prisoners standing to sue state authorities in federal court for civil rights violations under Title 42, U.S. Code, § 1983.[9]   Often called the "first modern prisoner's rights case,"[10] *Cooper v. Pate* (1964) is considered by many to mark the end of the judiciary's long-standing policy of non-intervention in penal governance and prisoners' rights issues. Indeed, in the five years immediately following the *Cooper* decision, the courts abandoned their embrace of the hands-off doctrine altogether and embarked on a course of massive intervention into the governance of American prisons that would last for more than two decades (Feeley & Rubin, 1998).

It was not long before the impact of the shift in judicial policy began to be felt by prison officials and prisoners alike. As Feeley and Rubin (1999) note, "As of 1964, no American court had ever ordered a prison to change its practices or its conditions."   One year later, however, the U.S. District Court in *Talley v. Stevens* (1965) declared certain conditions at Arkansas's Cummins Farm State Prison in violation of the Eighth Amendment ban on cruel and unusual punishment. Shortly thereafter, the court declared the entire facility unconstitutional and issued a series of injunctions aimed at restructuring the offending institution in accordance with its understanding of constitutional standards.[11]   Within five years, the court had declared the state's entire prison system in violation of the Eighth Amendment ban and placed it under comprehensive court order amounting to federal receivership.

Arkansas was only the first of many states to have its correctional system fall under the shadow of unconstitutionality. Indeed, by 1975 – only ten years after the *Talley v. Stephens* (1965) decision – specific prisons in half of the fifty United States, as well as the entire correctional systems of five of those states, had been declared unconstitutional and placed in receivership by the federal courts. In 1985, specific prisons in thirty-five states and nine entire prison systems were in federal receivership (Feeley & Rubin 1999).[12] Further, "in 1995, the ACLU estimated that prisons in forty-one states, as well as the District of Columbia, Puerto Rico, and the Virgin Islands" and at least some jails in all 50 states had at one time or another been under court order" (Feeley & Rubin 1999:13).

Growing awareness of the appalling conditions in American prisons led many U.S. justices to confront the question of when prison conditions are so inhumane that they violate the Eighth Amendment's ban on cruel and unusual punishments. Indeed, the 1970s and 1980s marked a period of increased responsiveness to prisoners' claims of unconstitutional prison conditions. Although judicial intervention brought many improvements in prison conditions and practices, "prison rape – the most widely and deeply feared aspect of imprisonment – [was] left to fester" (Robertson 2003). As an article in the *North Carolina Law Review* noted:

> In the meantime, the exploding prison population has diminished monitoring of inmates and created what Human Rights Watch describes as "a stronger incentive to pacify – rather than challenge – the more dangerous prisoners who may be exploiting others"[13] For a male behind bars, the bottom line reads: "prison authorities cannot protect his body's privacy (Robertson 2003).

Although prison rape was not "discovered" by the U.S. press until 1969, by that time the criminal courts had been dealing with sexual assault behind bars for some time. As an opinion handed down by the Supreme Court of Missouri indicates, "crimes against nature" and "sodomy" perpetrated behind carceral walls were prosecuted in U.S.

courts as early as 1915. Indeed, in *State v. Price* (1915), the defendant was charged with and convicted of "the detestable and abominable crime against nature."[14]   Found guilty of committing an "offense upon the body of an 18-year-old boy while the two were cellmates confined in the county jail at Independence, Missouri," Sterling was sentenced to an additional 10 years behind bars. The defendant appealed his conviction on the grounds that evidence presented at trial was insufficient to support the conviction. The Court found to the contrary and affirmed the lower court's verdict.

In the 1960s, the courts continued to adjudicate the "crime" of sodomy committed by prisoners. A 1963 case involving multiple appellants[15] illustrates the court's dilemma in prosecuting cases of carceral sodomy in which the "victim" was alleged to have cooperated in the perpetration of the "crime." In this case, defendant Douglas Theodore Henry was charged with aiding and abetting in the commission of "first degree sodomy"[16] – a crime of which he was also the alleged victim. The original charge read:

> The said Douglas Theodore Henry, on or about the 26th day of December, nineteen hundred and sixty-one, at the City of Syracuse, in this county, at the Cedar Street Jail on Cedar Street, did aid and abet one Thomas Dewey, a male person of the age of twenty-three years lawfully detained in said jail, to carnally know said Douglas Theodore Henry, who was then and there lawfully detained in said jail, by and with the mouth, in that said Douglas Theodore Henry counseled, induced and procured the said Thomas Dewey to place his mouth on and around the penis of the aforesaid Douglas Theodore Henry and did, therefore, commit the crime and felony of Sodomy as a principal as defined in § 2 of the Penal Law of the State of New York.[17]

In this case, the high court noted that "the indictment was complicated by charging that the defendant aided and abetted the other participant to carnally know the defendant, instead of directly charging that the defendant himself committed the crime of sodomy by carnally knowing Dewey."[18]   "A complication arises," the court observed, from the fact that:

According to the indictment, both Dewey and the defendant were "lawfully detained in jail" at the time of the commission of the act. Under subdivision 5 of § 690 of the Penal Law, if the person upon whom the crime is committed is "in the custody of the law, of any officer thereof, or in any place of lawful detention" the absence of his consent to the act is implied and therefore the person committing the act upon him is guilty of sodomy in the first degree, even though both were of full age and even though, in fact, both voluntarily participated. This provision makes Dewey's crime sodomy in the first degree but it is arguable that, by the same token, it makes the defendant a victim rather than an accomplice of the perpetrator of the crime, since by presumption of the law he is deemed to have been an unwilling participant. If this view is taken, the indictment may be insufficient insofar as it rests upon the theory that the defendant aided and abetted Dewey in the commission of the crime. We can, however, cut through this difficulty by treating the indictment as one charging directly that the defendant committed the crime of sodomy upon Dewey.[19]

In short, by virtue of their status as prisoners, each participant was legally incapable of consenting to sexual relations. Therefore, despite the fact both parties freely admitted to voluntarily participating in the sexual incident, in the eyes of the law, each could be found guilty of perpetrating forcible sodomy on the other.

DIAGNOSING THE PROBLEM

Crime

Twenty-six percent of the appellate opinions published in the historical period framed prison rape as a criminal offense. Almost exclusively, opinions that framed the phenomenon in these terms deployed a script representing prison rape as "a crime against nature" or "sodomy." For example, in *Hall v. State of Maryland* (1969)[20], the defendant appealed his conviction by the Circuit Court for Anne Arundel County, Maryland for "first degree sodomy" on a fellow prisoner. Hall argued that the trial court erred in admitting hearsay testimony and asserted that there was insufficient evidence to support the guilty verdict for a crime involving forcible compulsion. The Court of Special Appeals of Maryland found against the defendant on both points and affirmed his conviction. The case of *Lewis v. State of Oklahoma* (1969) was equally straightforward and was dealt with in a similar manner by the appellate court. Defendant Lewis appealed from a judgment of the District Court of Tulsa County which had found him guilty for the offense of first degree sodomy while incarcerated and sentenced him to three-to-nine years of additional imprisonment. Lewis was alleged to have "forced another cellmate in the county jail to permit him to commit oral sodomy on him."[21] The defendant alleged the lower court had abused its discretion in refusing to allow a continuance based on the absence of a witness for the defense who would have contradicted evidence of force. The court found to the contrary and affirmed both his conviction and his sentence.

Published not long after the decision in *Lewis, United States v. Brewer* (1973) is among the more interesting cases deploying the "crime against nature" script. In this case, "Alexander Paul Brewer, a convict at the Lewisburg Federal Penitentiary, was charged with assault with intent to commit sodomy and with the act of sodomy itself, in violation of the Pennsylvania Penal Code."[22] Having found the act in question to have been consensual, a jury acquitted Brewer of the assault count but convicted him on the charge of sodomy – a "crime" he freely admitted to having committed on more than one occasion while in prison.

Among the appellate opinions that comprise the data for this analysis, the court's opinion in *Brewer* is noteworthy for being the first to deploy the term "prison rape." Despite the fact that it remained a legal impossibility for one male to "rape" another, regardless of the venue in which an incident occurred, "prison rape" emerged for the first time in this 1973 opinion. Equally noteworthy is the defendant's initiation of a discourse challenging the constitutionality of states' ban on the practice of consensual sodomy among incarcerated individuals. Indeed, following his acquittal on the assault charge, defendant Brewer claimed "that he should be free to engage in [consensual] sodomy in prison" if he chose to do so.[23] The court's holding in the case amounted to the last word on the subject and remains the legal standard today. The United States District Court for the Middle District of Pennsylvania opined:

If the simple question of adult consensual sodomy were involved, this Court might strike down the statute.[24] However, the conduct of Alexander Paul Brewer occurred in prison, where the rationale for regulation of the conduct at issue is strong. While imprisonment results in the forfeiture of certain rights, it does not extinguish all claims to protection from unconstitutional or illegal regulation and procedure....Aside from the inevitable diminished right to privacy in prisons, there exists the need to regulate activities in prisons which in other settings would be unnecessary. Prison rapes are a serious problem. The psychological effect upon the victim may be serious and may reduce the chances of rehabilitation, slim as they are under present conditions. Perhaps forward-looking legislative and administrative reforms with respect to conjugal visits will alleviate the problem of prison rape. Considering the fact that inmates are in need of protection from sexual and other assaults encountered in prison, prohibition of consensual sodomy in prison cannot be viewed as unconstitutional legislation....The interest in preventing disorder in prison and injury to prisoners is sufficient to justify the existence of a prison regulation, or a state or federal statute, prohibiting consensual acts of sodomy between prison inmates. Two additional factors to be considered in balancing the state's interest in proscribing a prisoners conduct against asserted constitutional rights or privileges are: (1) the threats of violence which may cause a victim to "consent" to sodomy, and as a corollary, the difficulty in proof, and (2) the very tense and potentially dangerous situation existing within the prison confines as opposed to society at large. These additional factors convince the court that "consensual" sodomy between prison inmates may be validly prohibited.[25]

Brewer was not alone in challenging state-level statutes forbidding individuals from engaging in sodomy. Two subsequent cases heard by the Court of Appeals of Michigan, *People v. Coulter* (1980) and *People v. LaVictor* (1980) challenged the constitutionality of that state's sodomy statutes. In these cases, which were heard together:

"[d]efendants challenge[d] the constitutionality of the sodomy statute on three grounds: (1) vagueness in that the average person does not understand what is meant by "the abominable and detestable crime against nature"; (2) denial of equal protection because the statute treats male homosexual intercourse more harshly than female homosexual intercourse; and (3) overbreadth in that it prohibits conduct protected by the constitutional guarantee of privacy.[26]

As was the case in *U.S. v. Brewer* (1973), the court found it unnecessary to rule on the constitutionality of sodomy statutes in general. Responding to the appellants, the Michigan court noted, "We find it unnecessary to determine whether the sodomy statute infringes on the right to privacy of *all* adults.[27] We need only decide whether its application to adult prison inmates violates the constitutional guarantee of privacy."[28] In deciding both cases, the Michigan court "adopt[ed] the holding in *United States v. Brewer* [cited above]."[29]

Among the appellate opinions that framed prison rape as a crime, two others are worthy of note. First, in the case of *Patzka v. State of Alabama* (1985), a jury found the appellant guilty on an indictment that charged he had engaged in "deviate sexual intercourse with Daniel K. Thanum...in violation of §13A-6-63 of the Code of Alabama, which subsection (b) is classified as a Class A felony."[30] Already convicted of three previous felonies, Patzka was classified as a "habitual felony offender" in accordance with Alabama's Habitual Felony Offender Act of 1979 (No. 79-471). The legislative purpose and intent "in enacting the habitual offender statute were to prevent repetition and increase of crimes by imposing increased penalties upon repeat offenders" (Title 13A Criminal Code 1984 Edition, 13 A-5-9, p. 110).[31] By virtue of the provisions of the Act, Patzka's conviction on the charge of engaging in "deviant sexual intercourse by forcible compulsion" while incarcerated resulted in his sentencing to an additional term of life imprisonment without parole.

In the final year of the historical period, the California Court of Appeal published its opinion in *People v. Alford* (1991).[32] As was the case in the opinions described above, in *Alford*, prison rape was framed primarily as a crime. In contrast to the earlier cases, however, *People v. Alford* deployed an entirely new script. This case concerned a correctional officer convicted on three counts of sexual battery under

Cal. Penal Code § 243.4, and two counts of assault by a public official under color of authority pursuant to Cal. Penal Code § 149."[33] The trial court record indicates that, shortly before sexually assaulting them, Officer Alford placed two female inmates in restraints for the purpose of facilitating their transportation from one area to another. Based on the assertion that the women had originally been restrained for legitimate correctional purposes, Alford appealed his conviction of "sexual battery by restraint," a crime which, by definition, requires the *illegal* restraint of the victim. Describing the appellant's argument as "completely absurd," the Court of Appeals affirmed the lower court's verdict. The significance of Alford's case, however, lies less in its outcome than in its fact pattern. Indeed, in the context of this 1981 decision, a correctional officer emerged for the first time in the role of sexually violent perpetrator. This innovation was accompanied by another – the debut of "sexual misconduct," a term specifically used to denote sexual violence perpetrated by correctional staff members. The initial appearance of this script in the latter moments of the historical era rendered *U.S. v. Alford* (1991) unique among opinions published prior to 1992. However, after that time, cases deploying the sexual misconduct script appeared with increasing frequency. By the late 1990s, sexual misconduct amounted to the dominant discourse about prison rape in the appellate courts.

Sentencing Factor

A number of appellate opinions published prior to 1992 framed prison rape as a sentencing factor – one of the many elements that contribute to the determination of sentencing for particular individuals convicted of particular legally punishable behaviors. In essence, vulnerability to prison rape or alternatively, propensity for committing prison rape amounted to a way of knowing about particular individuals and how they would, or should, experience or impact a carceral environment. Cases that framed prison rape as a sentencing factor divided themselves among those relying on a script in which prison rape was a mitigating element in sentencing and those deploying a script in which it was an aggravating element. Among the former, a prisoner's past experience as a victim of sexual assault, or the perceived likelihood that the prisoner might be victimized while incarcerated in the future, was put forward as a mitigating factor – a reason to depart in a downward direction from applicable sentencing guidelines for specific crimes. Among the latter, a prisoner's record as the perpetrator of prison rape, or the likelihood that he might become a perpetrator in the future, was understood as an aggravating factor that called for the imposition of a harsher or more prolonged sentence than might otherwise have been imposed.

The court's opinion in *People v. Insignares* (1985) is representative of cases that relied on a script in which prison rape was construed as a mitigating factor. In this case, the Supreme Court of New York was asked to review a lower court's decision to grant a motion that not only set aside the defendant's conviction of narcotics trafficking, but also dismissed the indictment altogether based on the defendant's perceived vulnerability to sexual assault in prison. The action by the lower court was reversed based on the Supreme Court's following assessment of the circumstances:

> Criminal Trial Term abused its discretion by setting aside a verdict convicting defendant of criminal sale of a controlled substance in the second degree and dismissing the indictment upon the ground that such action was required in the interest of justice; although the 36-year-old defendant had no previous criminal record, was a community activist and businessman, and was allegedly raped while incarcerated awaiting sentencing, he was found guilty in the face of overwhelming evidence of selling almost two ounces of high quality cocaine for almost $4000 to an undercover agent and was negotiating a further sale of a pound of cocaine for $29,000. The trial court's discretion to dismiss in the interest of justice should be exercised sparingly and only in that rare and unusual case where it cries out for fundamental justice beyond the confines of conventional considerations, and those standards have not been met.[34]

In this case, the defense motion concentrated on a number of subjects, among which were the defendant's "good character" (an assessment that was founded on his community activism and his close family ties), as well as psychiatric evidence to the effect that, due to the psychological scars Insignares bore as a result of his alleged rape in prison, he would probably be unable to cope with further incarceration.

In addition, the defense focused on the likelihood that "the prison system would allegedly be unable to protect the defendant, who was physically small and allegedly nonaggressive, from sexual attacks by other inmates."[35]

In this and similar cases, the court was charged with determining whether, in the interest of equal justice, some compelling factor, consideration, or circumstance mandated downward departure from standard sentencing guidelines. In making this determination, the court weighed, among other things, the seriousness and circumstances of the defendant's offense, the harm caused by the offense, and the impact of a dismissal or downward sentencing departure on the public against the history, character and condition of the defendant. The court's June 25, 1985 opinion illustrates the outcome of the process in this particular case:

> We share the trail court's well-intentioned concern that prison inmates be protected from assault, including rape. Nevertheless, we hold that in the instant case, even if the defendant was, in fact, raped while incarcerated awaiting sentencing, such sexual assault is irrelevant to the defendant's jury conviction of the sale of almost two ounces of cocaine for nearly \$4000.[36]

In a similar case, *United States v. Tolias* (1977), the defendant appealed his sentence for "the crime of possessing stolen chattels, knowing them to have been stolen while in interstate commerce."[37] More simply put, Tolias stood convicted of possessing two fur coats allegedly stolen from a delivery truck in downtown Seattle, and was sentenced by the lower court to five year's imprisonment for the crime. In appealing his sentence, counsel claimed that the sentence was in violation of the Eighth Amendment ban on cruel and unusual punishment in that Tolias "is an admitted homosexual" and, as such, would be at increased risk for "assaults and homosexual rapes in prison."[38] In responding to Tolias's appeal, the court's opinion stated, "The test for cruel and unusual punishment is whether the penalty is so out of proportion to the crime committed that it shocks a balanced sense of justice. *Halprin v. United States*, 295 F.2d 458, 460 (9th Cir. 1961). We do not find that sentencing a homosexual to prison meets this test."[39] In the context then, prison rape was not considered irrelevant as it has been in Insignares (1985). Instead, the increased likelihood of prison rape was simply not understood to render the imposed punishment disproportionate to the crime.

In contrast to the opinions just described, another set of opinions published during this period relied on a script in which prison rape constituted an aggravating factor. In these cases, evidence of an individual's past experience as a perpetrator of sexual violence was considered relevant to the process of sentencing determination. Each of these cases involved an appellant convicted of capital murder and sentenced to death for the crime.

In the U.S. Supreme Court case of *Skipper v. South Carolina* (1986), the defendant stood convicted of murder and rape and was under sentence of death in South Carolina. At his sentencing hearing, the defendant's past good conduct and successful adaptation to a carceral environment was introduced as a mitigating factor. The defense intended to persuade the jury that if Skipper received a sentence of life in prison instead of death by execution, he could be expected to conduct himself in a non-violent manner in prison and that he would adapt successfully to a regime of incarceration.

Contradicting counsel's position, the prosecution submitted evidence aimed at convincing the trier of fact that Skipper's future conduct would be anything but adaptive. Indeed, the prosecution argued that, based on his past record as a rapist, Skipper "would be violent in jail, that he would rape other inmates."[40] In its opinion in the matter, the U.S. Supreme Court commented on the prosecutor's "extremely effective jury argument about, if you send this fellow to prison, he is going to rape other boy inmates in the jail because that is the kind of inmate he is, and you know that based on what you know about him, and on this record."[41]

Similarly, in the case of *Missouri v. Schlup* (1987), the appellant's alleged participation in a sexual assault was put forward as a means of knowing about him – that is, about the "kind of inmate" he would be. In Schlup, counsel strenuously objected to the submission of the testimony of the appellant's former cellmate, "who was the victim in the case involving appellant's second degree assault and sodomy convictions, alleged to be supportive of aggravating circumstances."[42] The cellmate's apparently inflammatory testimony was elicited by the State in the penalty phase of Schlup's trial to demonstrate aggravating circumstances in the form of "a substantial history of serious assaultive convictions."[43] The court was asked to determine, *inter alia*, whether the sentence of death was imposed under the influence of passion, prejudice, or any other arbitrary factor. In defending the lower court's admission of the cellmate's testimony, the court remarked:

> We cannot do other than concede to counsel that this witness had the base vocabulary required to most vividly and graphically describe a sexual assault involving participants of the same sex in prison surroundings. We would also remind counsel that we know of no way to describe sexual assaults involving male participants in prison surroundings which would not be both repugnant and repulsive to the ears of the ordinary listener or the eyes of the ordinary reader.

> We believe that when the legislature used the words "substantial history of serious assaultive criminal convictions," they contemplated there being presented to the jury something more than bare evidence of the conviction of the crime of "assault" or the bare conviction of some other crime which may include the element of assault. The jury is required to find a "substantial" history of "serious" assaultive criminal convictions. Assault can range from acts which constitute little more than conduct offensive to another to the most vile, sordid, repugnant and repulsive sexual assault upon the body of another. Sodomy can range from conduct between two consenting adults in the privacy of their own bedroom to the vile, sordid, repulsive conduct described in this record, conduct so base and vile that we believe there could be no social benefit from copying it in detail into this public opinion.[44]

At the end of the day, the court determined that the evidence presented was appropriate to support the finding of a statutory aggravating circumstance and was not intended to unduly inflame the passions of the jury against the defendant.

Regardless of their success or failure, these appeals illustrate how prison rape was rendered meaningful in the context of otherwise unrelated criminal proceedings. On one hand, past victimization, along with the alleged likelihood of similar future incidents, became a gauge for measuring the extent to which a particular prisoner might experience the punishment of incarceration. In these cases, the increased likelihood of sexual victimization in prison was alleged to constitute an extra, and therefore disproportionate, measure of punishment, potentially rendering the sentences handed down for vulnerable individuals unconstitutional. On the other hand, evidence that a prisoner had previously perpetrated prison rape was construed as a way of knowing about him or, more accurately, about his (in)ability to successfully adjust to the regime of incarceration. The perpetration of rape in prison was understood in this context to be indicative of an undesirable "type of prisoner." In many such cases, participation in the sexual assault of another prisoner often rose to become a primary consideration in determining whether a prisoner would be executed or live out his days in the cage.

Correctional Failure

No small number of historical era cases framed prison rape as an indication of correctional failure. By the late 1960s, the campaign of prison reform that had begun with the unraveling of the hands-off doctrine was winding down but it was by no means over. During the early years of this period, the courts remained entrenched, albeit to a lesser degree, in litigation aimed at reforming prisons. Opinions in cases related to prison reform litigation generally – in fact, universally – relied on an "unconstitutional conditions" script in discussing prison rape and other types of sexual abuse in U.S. prisons. According to this script, the high incidence and/or pervasive threat of prison rape amounted to evidence of conditions at particular institutions or across entire correctional systems that fell outside the bounds of constitutionality. Cases relying on this "unconstitutional conditions" script are discussed at length later in this section. Initially, however, a series of seven opinions is presented in which the relationship between prison rape and correctional failure was construed somewhat differently. Each of these opinions relates to the crime of escape from state custody and all seven cases (15.2% of the total cases published during this period) were published between 1969 and 1978. Opinions in these cases uniformly deployed a script that construed prison rape both as a sign of corrections' failure to protect prisoners of the state from harm and, simultaneously, as evidence of their failure at what may be their most fundamental mandated duty - to maintain secure and impermeable boundaries. In short, the threat of prison rape amounted – at least potentially – as an excuse for prisoners' escape from state custody.

The case of Wayne Robert Richards is the first in this seven-case "series."[45] On the morning of July 19, 1967, Richards, an inmate at the California Correctional Training Facility at Soledad, was assigned to a farm crew. Without permission, Richards left the area where he had been assigned to work sometime after 2:30 PM the same day, effectively escaping from incarceration. Richards hid in a cornfield until after dark and then proceeded to a main highway, where he caught a ride with a passerby to nearby King City. Still wearing prison attire, he was apprehended by police less than 12 hours later at a local service station.

Upon his return to prison, Richards was admonished as to his constitutional rights and interrogated by correctional personnel. When questioned as to the reason for his escape, Richards initially stated that "he felt he was doing too much time, that he was proceeding to Los Angeles to his mother's place to engage a lawyer to see if something couldn't be done."[46] At trial on the charge of escape, however, counsel offered a different account of events that led to Richards' escape:

> Ladies and gentlemen of the jury, you have heard what is called a prima facie case of escape. The law provides that in certain circumstances there are defenses to crimes....The law as to the various defenses will be stated to you by the Court. I will not attempt to state it. But the defense we are raising is called duress. Coercion. And we are going to present a series of witnesses, including the defendant himself, and these witnesses and the defendant will tell you of the threats made to his life and the reason why he ran away in order to save his own life, at least in his own mind he was doing this. And this will be the nature of our defense (269 Cal.App. 2d. 768: 770).[47]

Over objection, the defendant testified that for six months prior to his escape, he had been pressured by a group of prisoners to engage in "homosexual activity." Thereafter, outside the presence of the jury, he told the court that he had been forcibly sodomized during that time and that, "near to just prior" to escaping, he had again been forced to submit to "homosexual acts". Richards stated that reporting these incidents to officers at the facility resulted in no relief. However, as a result of his having "snitched" on the perpetrators, threats were made on his life. Five inmates approached him, showed him a piece of steel shaped like a knife and said, because he had "snitched" on their friends (the perpetrators of the prior rapes), Richards would be killed before the week was out unless he submitted to further acts of sodomy. Knowing of both the rapes and the threats against him prison officials did nothing, Richards testified. Consultations with a prison chaplain, a nurse, a doctor, and a head counselor each produced only suggestions that he "grow up and fight back" and a psychologist, who later testified that Richards was "a passive individual who has always had difficulty in expressing his masculinity and aggressive behaviour," offered the same advice. A correctional lieutenant suggested that Richards "find himself an old man to take care of him." Richards claimed that he had escaped to avoid further sexual assault and the threat of death, in his mind having exhausted every other possible remedy.

The court refused to receive the defendant's offer of proof on the proposed coercion defense and Richards was convicted of escape. He appealed, contending that the court had committed prejudicial error in disallowing such evidence and in refusing to give proffered instructions to the jury on coercion as justification for the charged offense. Based on § 26 of the California Penal Code, which provides (in part) that: "All persons are capable of committing crimes except those belonging to the following classes: ...Eight – Persons (unless the crime be punishable by death) who committed the act or made the omission charged under threats or menaces sufficient to show that they had reasonable cause to and did believe their lives would be endangered if they refused," the court of appeals unanimously affirmed the lower court's decision. "Submission to sodomy," the court averred, "abhorrent as it may be, falls short of loss of life."

In *People v. Noble* (1969), a factually similar case heard by the Court of Appeals of Michigan the same year, the majority again affirmed the conviction of escape from state custody, albeit on slightly different grounds. More important than the court's specific reasons for affirming Noble's conviction was its proffered solution to the problem of "homosexuality in the prisons," which, the court admitted, constituted a "serious and perplexing" problem:

Finally, defendant protests that he only fled the prison work
camp in desperation to avoid homosexual attacks by other
prisoners. The problem of homosexuality in the prisons is
serious and perplexing, and never more so than in a case such
as this where such activity is forced upon a young man against
his will. However, the answer to the problem is not the
judicial sanctioning of escapes. While we have no reason to
doubt the sincerity of this defendant, it is easy to visualize a
rash of escapes, all rationalized by unverifiable tales of sexual
assault. The solution must rather come from some kind of
penological reform.[48]

The case of *People v. Green* (1971) followed much the same
pattern as those just described. In the Green case, the defendant was
convicted of escape from the custody of the Missouri Department of
Corrections. Counsel tacitly conceded that, standing alone, the facts
sustained his conviction. However, Green also contended that his
escape was justified that that the justification constituted a legal
defense to the charge of escape. At pretrial, the defendant informed the
court that his defense to the charge of escape would be:

That prior homosexual assaults and threats near noon on the
day of his escape of a homosexual assault that night by other
inmates caused the conditions of his confinement to be
intolerable; and that these conditions, together with the state's
denial to him of access to the courts, made it necessary that he
escape in order to protect himself from submission to the
threatened assault or the alternative of death or great bodily
harm.[49]

In support of his argument, the defense offered the following:

The evidence offered on this issue is, in substance, that near
the end of December, 1966, shortly after defendant became an
inmate at the Training Center, he was attacked in his cell at
night by two inmates and submitted to acts of sodomy under
threat of death or great bodily harm; that immediately
thereafter he feigned an attempt at suicide and was taken to the
prison hospital where he told the authorities of the assaults and

asked to be removed from the institution to avoid further assault; that he was told by the Center authorities to resolve his own problems and to "go back and fight it out." Approximately two weeks later, near the middle of January, 1967, he was again homosexually assaulted in his cell, this time by three inmates. He again feigned an attempt at suicide and requested that he be taken to the hospital. Instead he was placed in a disciplinary cell until the next morning when he was x-rayed and immediately thereafter taken before the Disciplinary Board and charged with attempted self-destruction. He informed this Board of the assaults, requested protection, and was moved to another wing of the Training Center. He says that he was told by a member of the Board that he would have to "fight it out, submit to the assaults, or go over the fence." Approximately three months later, on April 14, 1967, during the noon hour, a group of four or five inmates told defendant that they would be at his cell that night and he would submit to their homosexual desires or they would kill or seriously harm him. He did not report the threat to anyone. He escaped at about 6:00 p.m. that evening.[50]

In essence, Green's appeal was based on his contention that the trial court had erred in excluding the offer of proof because:

> ...to do so violated due process in that it permitted appellant to be convicted and punished for escape even though [1] escape was his only means of obtaining access to the courts for a review of allegedly unconstitutional treatment, [and 2] the state made escape necessary for the appellant to protect himself from impending grave physical harm.[51]

In this case, the majority appears to have had even less sympathy for the appellant's situation than it had in the case of *People v. Richards* (1969) several years earlier. Indeed, in *Missouri v. Green*, the majority opinion stated:

> The principle of justification by necessity, if applicable, involves a determination that "the harm or evil sought to be avoided by such conduct is greater than that sought to be

prevented by the law defining the offense charged." The compulsion from the harm or evil which the actor seeks to avoid, should be present and impending.

This is not a case where defendant escaped while being closely pursued by those who sought by threat of death or bodily harm to have him submit to sodomy. Moreover, the threatened consequences of his refusal to submit could have been avoided that day by reporting the threats and the names of those making the threats to the authorities in charge....Defendant had several hours in which to consider and report these threats.

The defense of necessity was not available to defendant and the court did not err in excluding his offer of proof. Defendant's defense resolves itself into the simple proposition that the conditions of his confinement justified his escape. Generally, conditions of confinement do not justify escape and are not a defense.[52]

In contrast to the majority's summary rejection of Green's appeal, however, Justice Robert E. Seiler of the Supreme Court of Missouri saw Green's predicament in an entirely different light. Indeed, in his dissenting opinion Justice Seiler noted:

The evidence shows defendant was confronted with a horrific dilemma, not of his own making. No one, I am sure, wants to force a prisoner to live under conditions where he must either become a "punk" and debase himself, or a "snitch" at the risk of his life, but nevertheless this is the effect of our decision, until and unless the state improves the conditions in the prisons. I am not advocating that we should permit each prisoner to determine whether the conditions of his imprisonment justify an escape. What I am saying is that when the facts presented, if believed, would establish the defense of coercion, then this defense should be available to a charge of escape.

The perspective expressed in Justice Seiler's dissent highlights increasing concern among some members of the judiciary over the conduct of American corrections and foreshadows a number of majority opinions to follow. For example, in the case of *People v. Harmon* (1974), the court noted, "The time has come when we can no longer close our eyes to the growing problem of institutional gang rapes in our prison system." Accordingly, the court declined to follow the Noble Court's (see above) decision to disallow "the application of established defenses by prison inmates who escape to avoid homosexual attacks. While it is obvious that penal reform by the Legislature is the best solution to this difficult problem," the court continued, "we should not, because of that fact, preclude a defendant from presenting available defenses in the courts of this state." [53] Further, in *Harmon* the Court noted:

> The persons in charge of our prisons and jails are obliged to take reasonable precautions in order to provide a place of confinement where a prisoner is safe from gang rapes and beatings by fellow inmates, safe from guard ignorance of pleas for help and safe from intentional placement into situations where an assault of one type or another is likely to result. If our prison system fails to live up to its responsibilities in this regard we should not, indirectly, countenance such a failure by precluding the presentation of a defense based on those facts. [54]

Later the same year, a California court heard an appeal in the case of in *People v. Lovercamp* (1974), in which defendant Lovercamp and a co-defendant had been convicted of escaping from the California Rehabilitation Center "to avoid a threatened sexual assault by a group of lesbian prisoners." [55] As in the earlier cases, the defendant challenged her conviction on the escape charge, contending that the trial court erred in not allowing evidence in support of her necessity defense to be presented to the jury. Observing that, in the case before the court, it would be unrealistic "to expect the ladies to await effective 'penological reform,'" [56] the court reversed Lovercamp's conviction and clarified the rule in cases of escape on the basis of necessity. In essence, the court held that, under certain conditions, the defense of necessity *is* available to prisoners who escape. At the same time, the court hastened to add, "We do not conceive that we have created a new defense to an escape charge. We merely recognize, as did an English Court 238 years ago, that some conditions 'excuseth the felony.'"[57]

In addition to the cases just discussed, the opinions in certain civil rights-based class actions seem most at home among the cases that framed prison rape as an indicator of correctional failure than among the rights-related cases discussed in the following section. Indeed, in *Holt v. Sarver* (1970) and *Alberti v. Klevenhagen* (1985)[58] prison rape was framed both as a rights issue and as an indicator of the failure of corrections as an institution.

Holt v. Sarver (1970)[59] (*hereafter, Holt II*) consisted of eight prisoner-generated petitions that were consolidated and certified as a class action by Chief Judge Henley of the U.S. District Court for the Eastern District of Arkansas.[60] These actions were brought by inmates of the Cummins Farm Unit of the Arkansas State Penitentiary System and the Tucker Intermediate Reformatory against members of the Arkansas State Board of Corrections and the State Commissioner of Corrections. On behalf of themselves and on the behalf of future inmates of Cummins Farm and the Tucker Reformatory, the plaintiffs contended that practices and conditions at the two institutions were in violation of the Eighth, Thirteenth, and Fourteenth Amendments to the U.S. Constitution. Specifically, the inmates claimed: 1) that forced, uncompensated farm labor exacted from Arkansas convicts for the benefit of the State violated the Thirteenth Amendment ban on involuntary servitude; 2) that conditions and practices within the system were such that confinement there amounted to a cruel and unusual punishment proscribed by the Eighth Amendment; and 3) that unconstitutional racial segregation was practiced in violation of the Fourteenth Amendment. While the earlier *Holt v. Sarver* (1969) case,[61] along with *Talley v. Stevens* (1965) had focused on specific problems prevalent in the system, in *Holt II*, in effect, "confronted the entire structure, organization, philosophy, and consequences of the State's penal system" (Feeley & Rubin 2004:63). As Judge Henley noted, "As far as the Court is aware, this is the first time that convicts have attacked an entire penitentiary system in any court, either State or federal."[62]

In the context of Judge Henley's opinion in *Holt II*, prison rape and other forms of sexual assault occurring at Cummins Farm and were represented as indicators of the failure of the Arkansas penal system to operate within constitutionally mandated parameters. In *Holt v. Sarver I* (1969),[63] Judge Henley had noted:

> The Court recognizes, of course, that assaults, fights, stabbings, and killings may and do occur in penal institutions that are unquestionably well equipped, well staffed, and well managed. It occurs to the Court, however, that such incidents in such institutions take place in spite of all reasonable precautions taken by prison authorities. At Cummins there are no precautions worthy of the name, and the "creepers" and "crawlers"[64] take deadly advantage of that fact.

> The Court is of the view that if the State of Arkansas chooses to confine penitentiary inmates in barracks with other inmates, they ought to at least to be able to fall asleep at night without fear of having their throats cut before morning, and that the State has failed to discharge a constitutional duty in failing to take steps to enable them to do so.[65]

In *Holt v. Sarver II* (1970), he added:

> Conditions in those barracks have not changed significantly since *Holt I* was decided, except that there has been a decline in the rate of stabbings. There is, however, something more to be said about the barracks in the light of the evidence produced in this case.

> The Court heard much testimony about homosexuality in the barracks and elsewhere at Cummins. Homosexuality probably is practiced in all prisons in the United States, and there is a great deal of it practiced at Cummins, some consensual, a great deal nonconsensual. An inmate who is physically attractive to other men may be, and frequently is, raped in the barracks by other inmates. No one comes to his assistance; the floor walkers do not interfere; the trustees look on with indifference or satisfaction; the two free world people on duty appear to be helpless.

In an effort to protect young men from sexual assaults, they are generally assigned to the two rows of cots nearest the front bars of the barracks, which portion of the barracks is called "punk row." It appears, however, that if would-be assailants really want a young man, his being assigned to the "row" is no real protection to him.

Sexual assaults, fights, and stabbings in the barracks put some inmates in such fear that it is not unusual for them to come to the front of the barracks and cling to the bars all night. That practice, which is of doubtful value, is called "coming to the bars" or "grabbing the bars." Clearly, a man who has clung to the bars all night is in poor condition to work the next day.

Conditions in the barracks are worsened by the prevalent consumption of liquor and beer and by the use of drugs. It is not uncommon for many, if not all, of the inmates of a particular barracks to become intoxicated by drugs and alcohol all at the same time. The resulting commotion, violence, and confusion are quite imaginable. The free world people cannot control the situation; the trusties will not and are not supposed to; and the floor walkers frequently participate in the orgies.[66]

Clearly, in *Holt II*, sexual assaults constitute a significant part of the degradation and peril the judge found objectionable – and unconstitutional – at Cummins Farm. As Judge Henley noted in his opinion in this case:

Apart from the physical danger, confinement in the Penitentiary involves living under degrading and disgusting conditions. This Court has no patience with those who still say, even when they ought to know better, that to change those conditions would convert the prison into a country club; the Court has not heard any of those people volunteer to spend a few days and nights at either Tucker or Cummins incognito.

The peril and degradation to which Arkansas convicts are subjected daily are aggravated by the fact that the treatment which a convict may expect to receive depends not at all upon the gravity of his offense or the length of his term. In point of fact, a man sentenced to life imprisonment for first degree murder and who has a long criminal record may expect to fare better than a country boy with no serious record who is sentenced to a term of two years for stealing a pig.[67]

"However constitutionally tolerable the Arkansas system may have been in former years," Judge Henley averred, "it simply will not do today as the Twentieth Century goes into its eighth decade."

In *Judicial Policy Making and the Modern State*, Feeley and Rubin (1998:65) note that "[Judge] Henley's long catalog of abuses [among them, the incidence and pervasive threat of prison rape at Cummins Farm] and his rulings that they were unconstitutional constituted an attack on virtually every facet of the prison system." His broad ruling in the case "condemned the entire prison system and demanded immediate, accelerated efforts to transform it." In short, Judge Henley's opinion, later upheld by the Eighth Circuit Court of Appeals, required "a fundamental reorientation in the nature of the correctional system."

Rights

During the historical era, the line separating cases that framed prison rape primarily as an indication of correctional failure from those framing the phenomenon primarily as a rights issue was fuzzy at best. Indeed, as *Holt v. Sarver* and *Alberti v. Klegenhaven et al.* demonstrate, opinions that framed prison rape principally as an indication of correctional failure relied largely on a discourse of constitutional rights. Indeed, as the data revealed, opinions that framed prison rape principally as an indication of correctional failure clearly relied on a discourse of constitutional rights and, conversely, cases framing prison rape primarily as a rights issue drew heavily on a discourse about institutional failure.

Only a handful of opinions published in the historical period framed prison rape primarily as a rights-related issue. Among the few that did, the facts were dramatically different in each case. Nevertheless, they held in common a focus on prisoners' constitutional right to be protected from sexual assault while incarcerated. In *Little v. Walker* (1977), for example, plaintiff Malcolm Little, Jr. filed a civil rights, class suit under 42 U.S.C. § 1983 naming the Illinois

Department of Corrections, its director and former director, the Governor of Illinois, the Warden of Stateville Penitentiary and his predecessor, the Superintendent of Stateville Prison, among others as defendants. Little's complaint alleged that he and fellow inmates at Stateville "repeatedly suffered acts and threats of physical violence, sexual assaults, and other crimes perpetrated by other inmates from whom plaintiffs were not reasonably protected by defendants" and that inmates "lived in constant and imminent fear of physical violence and sexual assaults, 'especially when inflicted by gang-affiliated inmates.'"[68]

According to testimony published in the opinion of the Seventh Circuit Court of Appeals, the plaintiffs (each of whom was confined to the Segregation-Safekeeping Unit at Stateville) had their meals served by gang-affiliated inmates who withheld "meals from plaintiffs unless plaintiffs perform[ed] unnatural sexual acts through the cell bars. Defendants ignored plaintiffs' entreaties to remedy the situation."[69] Further, according to Little's complaint, on September 6, 1973, "through defendants' failure to afford reasonable protection, cell-house B was seized by a group of rebellious inmates for nine hours while gang rapes were inflicted on other inmates."[70] In short, Little claimed that he and other inmates were deprived of a number of their constitutional rights, including due process of law, equal protection of the laws, and freedom from cruel and unusual punishment. Further, Little alleged that the defendants acted with malice and reckless disregard for prisoners' rights by failing to provide ,reasonable protection from violent inmates and subjecting inmates in protective segregation to extreme deprivations. Based on evidence of the sexual assaults established during earlier proceedings, the court described Little's treatment as "so unreasonable as to be characterized as vindictive, cruel or inhuman, and intolerable in fundamental fairness that even the *Breeden* majority[71] would have found a violation of his constitutional rights."[72] Ultimately, the court found for the plaintiffs and remanded the case to a lower court for further proceedings.

The following year, in *Withers v. Levine* (1978), the plaintiff brought a civil rights action pursuant to 42 U.S.C. § 1983 seeking compensatory, declaratory, and injunctive relief against officials of the Maryland Division of Correction for failing to take reasonable measures to protect him from sexual assault. The facts of the case are as follows: On November 1, 1973, Withers had been placed in a two-man cell already occupied by Leon Redd. According to the plaintiff, on the night of November 2, 1973, at approximately 10:30 p.m. when the cell was locked, Redd held a razor blade to Withers' neck and forced him to submit to "homosexual activity." In this case, the court noted:

> While occasional isolated attacks among prisoners do not amount to cruel and unusual punishment, a prisoner has a right, through the Eighth and Fourteenth Amendments, to receive reasonable protection from harm by other inmates. Both actual assault and constant fear of assault are undue burdens to place upon a prisoner....The question for consideration now is whether the defendants have met their responsibility under the facts of the case. The conclusion is that they have not.[73]

Similarly, in *John Doe v. Swinson* (1976), the plaintiff sued Sheriff Swinson and various others individuals employed in the operation of the Fairfax Country, Virginia jail, seeking damages pursuant to 42 U.S.C. § 1983 for alleged denial of his constitutional rights to equal protection of the law and freedom from cruel and unusual punishment. John Doe, whose real name was William Wingfield, had been arrested and placed in custody at the Fairfax County Jail on February 7, 1975. Two days later, in the early morning hours of February 10, he was assaulted and raped on two separate occasions by three men sharing his cellblock. Despite the fact that Swinson and others testified that they were aware that sexual assaults on inmates were not uncommon at the facility, uncontradicted evidence indicated that there was no guard on the cell floor at the time of the attacks nor was there any sort of formal classification procedure in place at the jail to separate potentially dangerous felons from misdemeanants. In light of what the court found to be gross negligence on the part of Sheriff Swinson, the court affirmed the lower court's judgment in favor of the plaintiff in the amount of $50,000.

ATTRIBUTING BLAME

In the majority of appellate opinions published during this time period, attribution of blame for the problem of prison rape occurred on two levels. The factual narrative included in each case placed blame for prison rape on specific "types" of prisoners who perpetrated acts of sexual violence and on specific correctional officers whose negligence or malevolence contributed to the problem. At the same time, the judicial opinions laid blame for the problem at the doorstep of a dysfunctional correctional system that failed to adequately protect the prisoners in its custody.

Blaming Homosexuals and Homosexuality

Among the appellate opinions published during the historical time period, many deployed a script that attributed blame for prison rape to "homosexuals" or "homosexuality" – or in one case, to a "group of lesbians." Although the deployment of these scripts occurred across the entire 23-year period, cases published prior to 1980 were more likely to deploy the script than those published later.

Much of the discourse about prison rape circulated in appellate opinions stopped short of assigning blame for the problem on "homosexuals" *per se.* That is, the term "homosexual" was used primarily in adjectival form to describe a type of violent behavior rather than as a noun denoting a specific psycho-sexual identity. While male-on-male or female-on-female sexual assaults were understood as homosexual *practices* – namely, "homosexual attacks,"[74] "homosexual activity,"[75] "homosexual assaults,"[76] and "homosexual rape"[77] – perpetrators of these assaults were usually not identified as "homosexuals." In *People v. Noble* (1969), the judge observed, "That the defendant fled from prison to avoid homosexual attacks by other prisoners is not a defense to a charge of escape from prison."[78] Similarly, in *People v. Richards* (1969), the opinion stated, "The defendant brought out, over objection, that while at a conservation center camp between November 10, 1966 and March 28, 1967 he complained that there was pressure from other inmates to engage in homosexual activity." In the same case, it was noted that "the defendant informed the court that his defense would be that prior homosexual assaults, and threats near noon on the day of his escape of a homosexual assault upon him that night by other inmates, caused the conditions of his confinement to be intolerable.[79] For the most part, then, the term "homosexual" was associated more with sexual violence than sexual identity. Thus, Deputy Warden Dale Folz's testimony that "there definitely was a homosexual problem" at the institution he headed referred to the problem of sexual terrorism rather than the number of gay men incarcerated there.[80]

Although the above observations apply to the majority of cases published during this time period, they do not apply to all. In certain cases, there was some ambiguity as to the sexual identity of perpetrators of prison rape. *People v. Green* (1969), for example, observed that the defendant was forced to submit to other prisoners' "homosexual desires,"[81] a phraseology that appears to connote sexual identity more than violence or power. Other cases directly identified "homosexuals" as the perpetrators of carceral sexual assaults. *Wheeler v. Sullivan* (1984) contained testimony that "[t]he Task Team assigned to address the homosexual rape problem recognized that the presence of homosexuals and youthful offenders in the general population was a factor contributing to the problem."[82] Drawing heavily on the classic script of predatory homosexuals as spoilers of American youth, the court's observation clearly casts "homosexuals" as perpetrators of prison rape. Similarly, in *Roland v. Johnson* (1988), an overview of the facts of the case revealed that the alleged co-perpetrators of a rape had been reclassified "because of investigative reports linking them to an ongoing homosexual pressure gang in 11 Block, and because of hearsay evidence that Weatherspoon and Perry being homosexual predators is consistent with the evidence in their records, both in and out of prison."[83] It was also noted in this opinion that the victim's mother, Mrs. Jean Barry, notified the warden "that her son was in danger of being assaulted by homosexual predators," to which the warden responded that "if her son was not a homosexual, he had nothing to worry about."[84]

Interestingly, the opinion that most directly pointed the finger of blame at homosexuality involved female prisoners. In *People v. Lovercamp* (1974), an inmate at a California prison for women appealed her conviction on a charge of escape. Lovercamp and another women had admitted to going "over the wall" in order to avoid being sexually assaulted by a group of female prisoners at the institution. According to the defendant's testimony at trial:

> They had been in the institution about two and a half months and during that time had been threatened continuously by a group of lesbian inmates who told them they were to perform

lesbian acts or fight. They complained to authorities but nothing was done about their complaints, and on the day of the escape, 10 or 15 of these lesbian inmates approached them and again offered defendants the alternative of fighting or performing lesbian acts. A fight ensued, after which defendants were told by the group of lesbians that they 'would see the group again.'"[85]

Opinions in which "homosexuals" (or "lesbians") were directly identified as perpetrators were distributed fairly evenly across the entire time period and thus, the passage of time does not appear to have been correlated with the frequency with which homosexuals were identified as perpetrators. Indeed, *Lovercamp* (1974) was published quite early in the time period, while *Wheeler v. Sullivan* (1984) and particularly *Roland v. Johnson* (1988) appeared much later. It may well be that the wording of these opinions reflected the individual views and prejudices of their specific authors rather than any sort of trend in the legal representation of homosexuals as perpetrators of rape.

Blaming "Non-White" Prisoners

Relatively few appellate opinions attributed blame for sexual assaults directly to prisoners of color. Among those that did, however, the attribution was sometimes strikingly straightforward. For example, in *La Marca v. Turner* (1987), the court noted, "An experience repeated over and over in the testimony is the 'wolfing' and cat-calling by Black inmates to White inmates upon arrival of the latter group at GCI [Glades Correctional Institution]."[86] The following year, in *Vaughn v. Willis* (1988), the court record indicated, "The plaintiff in the complaint alleges that the guards' failure to afford the plaintiff protection from black gangs resulted in the beating and sexual assault of the plaintiff by gang members." In the same case, one rapist was identified as "a member of the Black Gangster Disciples Gang."[87] In *Schyska v. Shifflet et al* (1973) the court record noted that "[i]n late December, 1966, or early January, 1967, during the night, two black inmates picked the lock of defendants' cell door. At knifepoint, defendant was homosexually ravaged by both inmates.[88]

In contrast to these blatantly racialized attributions of blame for prison rape, in at least one instance, a connection between prisoners of color and the perpetration of rape was drawn more subtly. In a case discussed above, four members of the "Mickey Cobras Street Gang" were accused of raping a "white" inmate. While the connection to a street gang may suggest "non-whiteness" in and of itself, the African-American-ness of the rapists might only have been clearly apparent to readers familiar with the exclusively black membership of this particular gang. The identification of the victim as "white" constituted another indirect identification of the perpetrators as not white.

On the whole, the race of rapists and/or victims does not appear to have played a large role in the discourse about prison rape in appellate opinions published during this time period. This is not to say, however, that race may not have been a salient factor in the courtroom. Just as the press often communicated race non-verbally through the strategic use of photographic imagery, the presence of visually identifiable minorities in the courtroom may well have allowed race to play a role in the proceedings while rendering verbal communication of race unnecessary.

Blaming Correctional Personnel

A number of the opinions published during this time period placed at least partial blame for prison rape on the shoulders of correctional personnel. Indeed, more than half the historical era opinions published pointed an accusatory finger at corrections officers. This is not to say, however, that correctional officers were frequently identified as perpetrators of rape during this time period. They were not.[89] But in a number of opinions, the behaviors of corrections personnel – in particular their complacency, inaction, and indifference – were represented as factors that contributed to the problem. For example, in the first case published during this period, *People v. Richards* (1969), the defendant testified:

> "He reported his fears to a correctional lieutenant and was told to settle down and find himself an old man to take care of him; that on the Sunday prior to his escape on July 19th he reported his trouble to the chaplain and was advised to try to defend himself and fight his persecutors; that he did not seek further psychiatric help because consultations at the camp with a

nurse, a doctor, the head counselor and a psychologist had
produced only advice to grow up and fight back."[90]

Two years later, the opinion in *People v. Green* (1971) noted much
the same behavior on the part of correctional officers. In that case the
record indicated, "The prison official told defendant that the alternatives
were to defend himself, submit [to rape], or 'go over the fence.'"[91] In
reference to the negligent behavior of officers in response to an
inmate's fear of rape, the court stated in *People v. Richards* (1969),
"[U]nfortunately...it is possible for prison guards to subject prisoners to
abuses and serious injury unjustified by any disciplinary need."[92] Later,
the court cited the negligence of one officer in particular as a proximate
cause of a rape that occurred in a North Carolina facility. The
victim/plaintiff, who had recovered $7500 based on a lower court's
finding of negligence on the part of the officer in charge, found his
award doubled by the appellate judge, who noted:

> Officer Neal neglected his duty to make periodic checks to
> safeguard the inmates from dangerous conditions, e.g. sexual
> assaults. Officer Neal did not exercise reasonable care to
> maintain security and prevent assaults and conflicts between
> these problem inmates. Because these were problem inmates,
> it was foreseeable that they would be in conflict with each
> other and a hazard to each other. It was also foreseeable that
> sexual assaults were a hazard at the Youth Center and that was
> known to Officer Neal. Officer Neal should have reasonably
> foreseen that inmates might be assaulted by each other if he
> failed to make the usual periodic checks for security and
> safety maintenance. Officer Neal had knowledge of the need
> and legal duty to insure the adequate protection of the
> prisoners from violence and assaults and was negligent, when
> by simple exercise of proper care, the acts of violence
> complained of herein should or might have been forseen [sic]
> and prevented. The negligence of Officer Neal was a
> proximate cause of the sexual assault and battery suffered by
> the plaintiff.[93]

In the opinions published during this period, it was not so much the
negligence or indifference of correctional personnel but their

malevolence that was blamed for the problem of prison rape. In *Ober v. State of Louisiana* (1982), for example, the plaintiff claimed that "he was sexually molested and raped by three inmates over a three-hour period while the guard on duty watched."[94] Similarly, in *Villante v. Department of Corrections of New York* (1986), for example, the court record indicated:

> Although Villante alleged a series of sexual assaults continuing over a period of about one month, his amended complaint focused on attacks allegedly occurring on November 22, 24, and 27, 1980. In a later disposition, Villante said that several inmates saw him being dragged from the prison dayroom to the cell where the attacks occurred and that certain inmates saw the forced acts of sodomy as well. He said that he made repeated complaints about the assaulting inmate to a corrections officer he identified as Marcelly and that he asked Marcelly to lock the door of his cell to prevent the attacks, but that Marcelly only laughed and opened the cell door.[95]

In another case heard two years later, a correctional officer was alleged to have "affirmatively aided and abetted" in the perpetration of multiple incidents of rape against a prisoner at Stateville Correctional Center in Joliet, Illinois. In this case, plaintiff Vaughn alleged:

> Shortly after being transferred to the protective unit on April 2, 1983, [he] was raped by four inmate-members of the "Mickey Cobras street gang."[96] Mr. Vaughn testified, over Mr. Willis' [the correctional officer] denial, that Mr. Willis forced him into a cell where two inmates raped him. Mr. Willis then returned Mr. Vaughn to his own cell and allowed two other inmates to rape him. A subsequent medical examination confirmed that Mr. Vaughn had been sodomized.[97]

Although such cases were uncommon in the historical period, there were opinions that clearly identified correctional officers as the perpetrators of prison rape. Having said this, it should be noted that two of these cases, *Hernandez v. Denton et al.*, (1988) and *Hernandez v. Denton et al.* (1990) are notorious in the annals of "factually frivolous" lawsuits. In fact, the plaintiff's allegations likely speak far more to his own mental illness than to the actions of either correctional officers or other prisoners. Indeed, much of what has been written about these two cases concerns the power of the courts to dismiss those claims whose factual contentions are "clearly baseless."[98] Nevertheless, many pages of legal opinion have been written on these cases in this (and the next) time period and cannot not be entirely dismissed based on their factual improbability.

Briefly, the plaintiff in these cases brought suit under 42 U.S.C. § 1983, claiming, among other things,[99] that he had been drugged and homosexually raped on 28 separate occasions by both correctional personnel and other inmates and that these events had occurred at several different correctional facilities. In fact, Hernandez did not identify any of the alleged perpetrators in his complaints – because he did not claim any direct recollection of the events. Rather, he asserted that he found what he believed to be needle marks on different parts of his body, and fecal and semen stains on his underwear, which led him to believe that he had been drugged and raped while he slept. Ultimately, in the next time period (1992), Hernandez's case would reach the U.S. Supreme Court, which was asked to rule on the power of the courts to determine when a case can be dismissed because it "lacks an arguable basis in either law or fact."[100]

Finally, in the last year of this time period, the case of *People v. Alford* (1991) (discussed earlier in this chapter) was heard by the Court of Appeal of California. In this case, William Lee Alford, a correctional officer was convicted of three counts of sexual battery under Cal. Penal Code § 243.4 and two counts of assault by a public official under color of authority pursuant to Cal. Penal Code § 149."[101] According to the uncontested facts of the case, the defendant sexually assaulted two female prisoners in his charge after placing them in restraints for transportation from one facility to another. Because the statutory definition of the crime stipulates an "unlawfully restrained" victim, Alford appealed his conviction on the "sexual battery" charges, arguing that his victims had *originally* been restrained lawfully. Describing Alford's argument as "utterly absurd," the court denied the appeal[102]

In the context of this discussion, it is interesting to note that, during this period, a number of cases that initially identified negligent, indifferent, or malevolent correctional officers as the *proximate* cause of prison rape ultimately placed the real blame for the problem on the doorstep of the correctional system. The most striking example of this attribution occurred in *Villante v. Department of Corrections of the City of New York* (1986). In this case the court averred, "[E]vidence that on several occasions no less than five named corrections officers watched and did nothing while the assailant was forcibly dragging Villante away to his lair certainly would tend to prove that there had been a gross failure in those officers' training."[103]   Along these same lines, in *Wheeler v. Sullivan* (1984), the court attributed the blame for correctional officers' complicity in, and complacency about, prison rape to the failures of the correctional system:

> Present correctional staff require professionalization in several areas including, but not limited to, recruitment, compensation, retention etc. It is fair to say that although the complicity and complacency of the correctional officers' staff is possibly the largest sole contributor to the present security lapses in the prison system, and it is equally true that the system's failure to provide management with sufficient tools to effectively deal with personnel problems in this area is also a contributor to the security problem. [104]

Blaming "The System"

Judicial opinions published during this period frequently deployed a script placing some measure of blame for the problem of carceral rape on a dysfunctional correctional system (as a whole). In fact, nearly 70% of the opinions published in the historical period placed blame for prison rape either wholly or partially at the doorstep of corrections[105] In general, the authors of these opinions painted corrections with broad strokes, attributing blame to the sort of fundamental failures so commonly associated with corrections they often seem to constitute "the nature of the beast": the lack of meaningful opportunity for rehabilitation; the rampant and largely unchecked violence within prison walls; the inability and/or unwillingness to maintain a minimum standard of decency and safety to the prisoners in their charge.   In appellate court discourse, the magnitude of corrections many failures frequently rendered them constitutionally significant.   In these cases, correctional failures were often held up to the light of "evolving standards of decency," becoming morally as well as practically problematic. In the court's opinion in *Holt v. Sarver* (1970) offers perhaps the most outstanding condemnation of a state's prison system to date. In considering the matter of injunctive relief for the multitude of correctional sins occurring within the confines of Arkansas' correctional institutions, the court averred:

> For the ordinary convict a sentence to the Arkansas Penitentiary today amounts to a banishment from civilized society to a dark evil world completely alien to the free world, a world that is administered by criminals under unwritten rules and customs completely foreign to free world culture....Such confinement is inherently dangerous. A convict, however cooperative and inoffensive he may be, has no assurance whatever that he will not be killed, seriously injured, or sexually abused. Under the present system, the State cannot protect him...It is one thing for the State to send a man to the Penitentiary as punishment for a crime. It is another thing for the State to delegate the governance of him to other convicts, and to do nothing meaningful for his safety, well being, and possible rehabilitation. It is one thing for the State to not pay a convict for his labor; it is something else to subject him to a situation in which he has to sell his own blood to pay for his safety....However constitutionally tolerable the Arkansas system may have been in former years, it simply will not do today as the Twentieth Century goes into its eighth decade.[106]

The court's opinion in *Alberti v. Klevenhagen* (1985) offered an equally scathing assessment of certain of Texas' correctional facilities:

> The physical conditions of both facilities, their physical design, and their manner of operation have resulted in conditions that can only be classified as cruel and inhuman under any current standards concerning human decency. Inmate beatings and homosexual rapes and attacks are prevalent. Inmates without any homosexual tendency have been forced by other stronger inmates to perform acts of oral sodomy as well as anal intercourse. Many of these attacks

have endured for long periods at a time. Among the female inmates, unwelcomed lesbianism is apparent....[G]iven the procedural history of this case, the evidence presented at the hearings over the course of the last twelve years, and the memoranda submitted concurrent with these motions, it has become clear that the defendants not only have failed to abide by the constitutional mandate, the Court's Order, or their own Consent Judgment to provide a safe and suitable jail, but have no intention of doing so. Such an affront to the public interest should not and cannot be tolerated by this Court...[107]

Although the courts heard scores of similar cases during this time period, relatively few cases rose to the constitutional magnitude of *Holt v. Sarver* and *Alberti v. Klevenhagen*. Nevertheless, opinions that attributed blame for prison rape to the prison system were no less clear about where the blame for prison rape should be placed. For example, in *People v. Unger* (1975), the court noted:

"This case involves an issue which is becoming increasingly significant by reason of the apparent inability of prison authorities to control the actions of inmates who are criminally assaulting other inmates with sexual assaults and other acts of violence....It was clear from the testimony of the State's witnesses that homosexual activities occurred in the prison, including sexual assaults on unwilling inmates (and even upon the prison doctor) and that there were 'gangs' of inmates perpetrating such assaults. The prison system apparently has not been able to provide complete security to the prisoners. [108]

Similarly, in *People v. Trujillo* (1978), the judge observed:

Indeed, the State has a duty to assure inmate safety....[O]ur prisons and jails are obliged to take reasonable precautions in order to provide a place of confinement where a prisoner is safe from gang rapes and beatings by fellow inmates....If our prison system fails to live up to its responsibilities in this regard, we should not, indirectly, countenance such a failure by precluding the presentation of a defense based on those facts.[109]

During the latter years of this period – specifically from 1984 through 1991 – the courts were less inclined to attribute blame for prison rape to systemic failures of a malignant institution and more apt to blame specific inadequacies within an otherwise functional – or at least potentially functional – penal system. For example, in 1984, the Wheeler Court pointed not to a morally offensive correctional system in utter disarray, but to four specific areas in which dysfunctional policies and management deficiencies were construed as "proximate causes of homosexual rape." Specifically, these included: 1) inadequate training of guards; 2) inadequate orientation of new inmates; 3) irresponsible classification practices; and 4) "extraordinarily reckless" practices with respect to the reporting, investigation, and prosecution of homosexual rapes.[110] Similarly, in 1985, the court stated:

> ...the high level of violence, sexual assault, and inmate control could not be attributed to one source. Rather, inadequate staffing levels, inadequate supervisory techniques, a poor physical design, and an unreliable communications system all contributed to the problems found in both facilities.[111]

The shift in how the system was understood to be at fault for prison rape was coincident with what Feeley and Rubin (1998) identify as a decline or "winding down" of prison reform in general. Indeed, by this time, many members of the judiciary felt that the most egregious conditions in American prisons had already been eliminated. Additionally, the civil rights movement – the engine driving much of the social reform accomplished in preceding decades – had largely run its course. A new political ethos prevailed in was less than supportive of rights-litigation as a source of social change. Increasingly, the challenges of corrections were being addressed administratively. It may be that the shift in the attribution of blame from the entire correctional system to specific administrative policies and managerial practices was a manifestation of the larger social and political changes that characterized the latter years of this time period.

[1] The term "hands off doctrine" is reported to have originated in Fritch, M. 1961. "Civil Rights of Federal Prison Inmates." Prepared for the Federal Bureau of Prisons.

[2] *Cornell v. State*, 74 Tenn. 624, 629 (1881).

[3] *Banning v. Looney*, 213 F.2d 771 (10th Cir.), 348 U.S. 859 (1954).

[4] *Ruffin v. Commonwealth*, 62 Va. 790, 794-96 (1871), for example, states:

> For the time being, during his term of service in the penitentiary, [the prisoner] is in a state of penal servitude to the State. He has, as a consequence of his crime, not only forfeited his liberty, but all his personal rights except those which the law in its humanity accords to him. He is for the time being the slave of the State.

[5] *Coffin v. Reichard*, 143 F.2d 443 (6th Cir. 1944).

[6] *Robinson v. State of California*, 370 U.S. 660 (1962).

[7] *Jones v. Cunningham*, 371 U.S. 236 (1963).

[8] *Cooper v. Pate*, 378 U.S. 546 (1964).

[9] The Civil Rights Act of 1871 is found in Title 42, § 1983 of the United States Code and is commonly referred to as § 1983. It provides that anyone who, under color of state or local law, causes a person to be deprived of rights guaranteed by the U.S. Constitution, or federal law, is liable to that person. The document reads:

> Every person who under color of any statute, ordinance, regulation, custom, or usage, of any State or Territory or the District of Columbia, subjects, or causes to be subjected, any citizen of the United States or other person within the jurisdiction thereof to the deprivation of any rights, privileges, or immunities secured by the Constitution and laws, shall be liable to the party injured in an action at law, Suit in equity, or other proper proceeding for redress, except that in any action brought against a judicial officer for an act or omission taken in such officer's judicial capacity, injunctive relief shall not be granted unless a declaratory decree was violated or declaratory relief was unavailable. For the purposes of this section, any Act of Congress applicable exclusively to the District of Columbia shall be considered to be a statute of the District of Columbia.

[10] Jacobs, James. 1983. "The Prisoners' Rights Movement and Its Impact," in *New Perspectives on Prisons and Imprisonment*, 33, 36 (J. Jacobs, ed., 1983) quoted in Feeley, Malcolm and Edward L. Rubin. 1999. *Judicial Policy Making and the Modern State: How the Courts Reformed America's Prisons*. Cambridge, UK: Cambridge University Press.

[11] See *Talley v. Stephens*, 247 F. Supp. 683 (E.D. Ark. 1965).

[12] Feeley and Rubin note: "[I]n 1995, the ACLU estimated that prisons in forty-one states, as well as the District of Columbia, Puerto Rico, and the Virgin Islands, had at one time or another been under court order." (p.13).

[13] Human Rights Watch. 2001. *No Escape: Male Rape in U.S. Prisons*. http://www.hrw.org/reports/2001/ prison/ report.html).

[14] *State v. Price*, 263 Mo. 276; 1915 Mo. LEXIS 145 (1915).

[15] *People of the State of New York v. Henry; People of the State of New York v. Rougeaux; People of the State of New York v. Deemer; People of the State of New York v. Buffington; People of the State of New York v. Edwards*; 18 A.D.2d 293; 239 N.Y.S.2d 146 (1963).

[16] Sodomy in the first degree requires "a non-consenting victim."

[17] Ibid.

[18] Ibid.

[19] Ibid.

[20] *Hall v. Maryland*, 5 Md. App. 599; 249 A.2d 217 (1969).

[21] *Lewis v. State of Oklahoma*, 1969 OK CR 295; 42 P.2d 336 (1969)

[22] *U.S. v. Brewer*, 363 F. Supp. 606; 1073 U.S. Dist. LEXIS 12065 (1973).

[23] Ibid.

[24] This based on the court's opinion that: "While there has been no Supreme Court decision on the precise issue of the constitutional validity of statutes aimed at preventing "deviant sexual conduct," the apparent trend of recent decisions would indicate that such a right among or between consenting adults does exist."

[25] Ibid.

[26] *People v. Coulter; People v. LaVictor*, 94 Mich. App. 531; 288 N.W.2d 448; 1980 Mich. App. LEXIS 2394 (1980).

[27] Italics in original.

[28] Ibid.

[29] Ibid.

[30] *Patzka v. State*, 481 So. 2d 438; 1985 Ala. Crim. App. LEXIS 5881 (1985).

[31] Ibid.

[32] *People v. Alford*, 235 Cal. App. 3d 799; Cal. App. LEXIS 1264 (1991).

[33] Ibid.

[34] *People v. Insignares*, 109 A.D.2d 221; 491 N.Y.S.2d 166; 1985 N.Y. App. Div. LEXIS 49742 (1985).

[35] Ibid.

[36] Ibid.

[37] *United States v. Tolias*, 548 F.2d 277; 1977 U.S. App. LEXIS 10630 (1977).

[38] Ibid.

[39] Ibid.

[40] *Skipper v. South Carolina*, 1986 U.S. TRANS LEXIS 99 (1986).

[41] Ibid.

[42] *Missouri v. Schlup*, 724 S.W.2d 236; 1987 Mo. LEXIS 264 (1987).

[43] Ibid.

[44] Ibid.

[45] The seven cases in this "series" include: 1) *People v. Richards*, 269 Cal. App. 2d 768; 1969 Cal. App. LEXIS 1698 (1969); 2) *People v. Noble*, 18 Mich. App. 300; 1969 Mich. App. LEXIS 1061 (1969); 3) *Missouri v. Green*, 470 S.W.2d 565; 1971 Mo. LEXIS 928 (1971); 4) *People v. Harmon*, 53 Mich. App. 482; 1974 Mich. App. LEXIS 1161 (1974); 5) *People v. Lovercamp*, 43 Cal. App.3d 823; 1974 Cal. App. LEXIS 1359 (1974); 6) *People v. Unger*, 33 Ill. App. 3d 770; 1975 Ill. App. LEXIS 3240 (1975); 7) *People v. Trujillo*, 41 Colo. App. 223; 1978 Colo. App. LEXIS 691 (1978).

[46] *People v. Richards*, 269 Cal. App. 2d 768, 75 Cal. Rptr. 597; 1969 Cal. App. LEXIS 1698 (1969).

[47] Ibid.

[48] People v. Noble, 18 Mich. App. 300; 1969 Mich. App. LEXIS 1061.

[49] *State v. Green*, 470 S.W.2d 565; 1971 Mo. LEXIS 928 (1971).

[50] Ibid.

[51] Ibid.

[52] Ibid.

[53] *People v. Harmon*, 53 Mich. App. 482; 1974 Mich. App. LEXIS 1161.

[54] Ibid.

[55] *People v. Lovercamp*, 43 Cal. All. 823; 1974 Cal. App. LEXIS 1359.

[56] Ibid.

[57] *People v. Lovercamp*, 43 Cal. All. 823; 1974 Cal. App. LEXIS 1359; See also 1 Hale P.C. 611 (1736).

[58] See *Alberti et al. v. Klevenhagen*, 606 F. Supp. 478 ; 1985 U.S. Dist. LEXIS 20911 (1985). For the sake of brevity, only *Holt v. Sarver* (1970) will be

discussed in detail in this section. *Alberti* (1985) is discussed at some length in a later section.

[59] The case was also known as "*Holt v. Sarver II*," to distinguish it from an earlier (1969) case involving the same defendants and plaintiff.

[60] Judge Henley had also been the presiding justice in the case of *Talley v. Stevens* (1965) discussed earlier in this chapter.

[61] Also known as "*Holt v. Sarver I* (1969)."

[62] *Holt v. Sarver*, 309 F.Supp. 362; 1970 U.S. Dist. LEXIS 12802.

[63] Prison rape was not mentioned in "*Holt v. Sarver I*" and, thus, the case is not included in the data set analyzed in the context of this research.

[64] The terms "creepers" and "crawlers" are defined in *Holt v. Sarver I*: "At times deadly feuds arise between particular inmates, and if one of them can catch his enemy asleep it is easy to crawl over and stab him. Inmates who commit such assaults are known as 'crawlers' and 'creepers.'"

[65] *Holt v. Sarver*, 300 F. Supp. 825 (E.D. Ark. 1969).

[66] *Holt v. Sarver*, 309 F.Supp. 362; 1970 U.S. Dist. LEXIS 12802 (1970).

[67] Ibid.

[68] *Little v. Walker et al.*, 552 F.2d 193; 1977 U.S. App. LEXIS 14134 (1977).

[69] Ibid.

[70] Ibid.

[71] See *Breeden v. Jackson*, 457 F.2d 578, 580 (4ᵗʰ Cir. 1972). In *Breeden v. Jackson* (1972) the majority denied equitable relief and damages to a prisoner confined in maximum security based on the fact that his complaints only "related to limited recreational or exercise opportunities, the prison menu, and restricted shaving and bathing privileges." The court described Little's privations at Stateville as "in sharp contrast" to those experienced by the plaintiff in *Breeden*.

[72] *Little v. Walker et al.*, 552 F.2d 193; 1977 U.S. App. LEXIS 14134 (1977).

[73] *Withers v. Levine* et al., 449 F. Supp. 473; 1978 U.S. Dist. LEXIS 18212 (1978).

[74] *People v. Noble*, 18 Mich. App. 300; 1969 Mich. App. LEXIS 1061 (1969).

[75] *Ibid.*

[76] *People v. Green*, 470 S.W.2d 565; 1971 Mo. LEXIS 928 (1971).

[77] *Wheeler v. Sullivan*, 599 F. Supp. 630; 1984 U.S. Dist. LEXIS 21794 (1984).

[78] *People v. Noble*, 18 Mich. App. 300; 1969 Mich. App. LEXIS 1061 (1969).

[79] *People v. Richards*, 269 Cal. App. 2d 768; 1969 Cal. App. LEXIS 1698 (1969).

[80] *Wheeler v. Sullivan*, 599 F. Supp. 630; 1984 U.S. Dist. LEXIS 21794 (1984).

[81] *People v. Green*, 470 S.W.2d 565; 1971 Mo. LEXIS 928 (1971).

[82] *Wheeler v. Sullivan*, 599 F. Supp. 630; 1984 U.S. Dist. LEXIS 21794 (1984).

[83] *Roland v. Johnson; Phillips; Foltz; and Toland*, 856 F.2d 764; 1988 U.S. App. LEXIS 12226 (1988).

[84] Ibid.

[85] *People v. Lovercamp*, 43 Cal. App. 3d 823; 1974 Cal. App. LEXIS 1359 (1974).

[86] *La Marca v. Turner*, 662 F. Supp. 647 ; 1987 U.S. Dist. LEXIS 10598 (1987).

[87] Ibid.

[88] *Schyska v. Shifflet et al.*, 364 F. Supp. 116 ; 1973 U.S. Dist. LEXIS 12016 (1973).

[89] With the exception of *Hernandez v. Denton, et al.* (1988) and *Hernandez v. Denton et al.* (1990), which will be discussed later in this section, in only one opinion published prior to 1992 was a correctional officer accused of raping a prisoner (see *People v. Alford*, 235 Cal. App. 3d 799; 1991 Cal. App. LEXIS 1264).

[90] *People v. Richards*, 269 Cal. App. 2d 768; 1969 Cal. App. LEXIS 1698 (1969).

[91] *People v. Green*, 470 S.W.2d 565; 1971 Mo. LEXIS 928 (1971).

[92] *People v. Richards*, 269 Cal. App. 2d 768; 1969 Cal. App. LEXIS 1698 (1969).

[93] *Taylor v. North Carolina Department of Corrections*, 88 N.C. App. 446; 1988 N.C. App. LEXIS 41 (1988).

[94] *Ober v. State of Louisiana*, 424 So. 2d 533; 1982 La. App. LEXIS 8702 (1982).

[95] *Villante v. Department of Corrections of the City of New York*, 786 F.2d 516; 1986 U.S. App. LEXIS 23252 (1986).

[96] The Mickey Cobras are a large street gang affiliated with the nationwide gang known as the People Nation. The Mickey Cobras are based in Chicago and comprised exclusively of African-American membership.

[97] *Vaughn v. Willis*, 853 F.2d 1372; 1988 U.S. App. LEXIS 10883 (1988).

[98] *Hernandez v. Denton, et al.*, 504 U.S. 25 ; 1991 U.S. LEXIS 2689 (1991).

[99] For example, Mr. Hernandez claimed that his Eighth Amendment rights had been violated based on the alleged fact that he slept without a blanket for one night!

[100] *Hernandez v. Denton, et al.*, 504 U.S. 25 ; 1992 U.S. LEXIS 2689 (1992).

[101] *People v. Alford*, 235 Cal. App. 3d 799; 286 Cal Rptr. 762; 1991 Cal. App. LEXIS 1264 (1991).

[102] Ibid.

[103] *Villante v. Department of Corrections of the City of New York*, 786 F.2d 516; 1986 U.S. App. LEXIS 23252 1986).

[104] *Wheeler v. Sullivan*, 599 F. Supp. 630; 1984 U.S. Dist. LEXIS 21794.

[105] It should be noted that this total includes the opinions in which the correctional system was blamed for the actions of "improperly trained" personnel in its employ (see preceding section, "Blaming Correctional O.

[106] *Holt v. Sarver*, 309 F. Supp. 362; 1970 U.S. Dist. LEXIS 12802 (1970).

[107] *Alberti et al. v. Klevenhagen*, 606 F. Supp. 478 ; 1985 U.S. Dist. LEXIS 20911 (1985).

[108] *People v. Unger*, 33 Ill. 3d 770; 1975 Ill. App. LEXIS 3240 (1975).

[109] *People v. Trujillo*, 41 Colo. App. 223; 1978 Colo. App. LEXIS 691 (1978).

[110] *Wheeler v. Sullivan*, 599 F. Supp. 630; 1984 U.S. Dist. LEXIS 21794.

[111] *Alberti et al. v. Klevenhagen*, 606 F. Supp. 478 ; 1985 U.S. Dist. LEXIS 20911 (1985).

CHAPTER FIVE

Prison Rape in the Courts, 1992-2006

INTRODUCTION

By the end of the 1980s, the momentum of the prison reform movement had slowed and prison conditions litigation in particular was in sharp decline. Feeley and Rubin (1998) cite a number of factors that contributed to the decline of the reform movement at this time. First, the successes the movement enjoyed led many to acknowledge that the most egregious correctional abuses had already been eliminated and that future challenges would be better addressed through administrative and managerial efforts than continued litigation and judicial intervention. Further, by this time, the rights revolution had largely run its course. Recent shifts in the political environment produced a climate that was less than favorable for an ongoing politics of rights – particularly prisoners' rights – and less than supportive of rights litigation as an avenue of social change. And finally, the wave of law-and-order politics that swept the nation in the 1970s and '80s and public concern over rising crime rates translated into an increasingly punitive social mood and a growing expectation that the power of the judiciary should be used to fill prisons, not to improve them.

The overall decline in prison-conditions litigation in the lower courts occurred in conjunction with the Supreme Court's reassessment and retrenchment of many rights and reforms that had been litigated during the preceding decades (Feeley & Rubin 1998). Throughout 1990s, the Court continued to hand down decisions effectively curtailing constitutional guarantees established as a part of the lower courts' experiment in "hands-on" prison reform. Indeed, prisoners' rights to free speech, due process, legal access, and free exercise of religion were all abridged to varying degrees as the high court endeavored to undo much of what the lower courts had accomplished in preceding decades (Feeley & Rubin, 1998).

Coincident with the Court's retrenchment of established rights and reforms, an increasingly tough-on-crime Congress passed legislation that further curtailed prisoners' rights, as well as their ability to access to the courts. In 1996, Congress passed the Prison Litigation Reform Act of 1995 (PLRA),[1] ostensibly to stem the rising tide of "frivolous," litigation clogging the courts. Among the provisions included in the PLRA, prisoners' ability to sue for rights violations in federal court was made contingent on their ability to show prior exhaustion of all available administrative remedies. In addition, the law established "public necessity" and "changing circumstances" as legal grounds for non-compliant correctional authorities to reopen the provisions of consent decrees to which they had previously committed.[2] A particular burden for many victims of prison rape, the Act also contained a provision barring prisoners from bringing federal action for "mental or emotional injury suffered while in custody without a prior showing of physical injury."

While prison-conditions litigation in general may have been on the decline, contemporary era courts were increasingly occupied handing down decisions related to prison rape. During the 15-year period from 1992 through 2006, the appellate courts published a total of 122 opinions relevant to sexual violence in prisons, almost three times the number published annually in the preceding period. The opinions published after 1991 represent about 73% of the total published across the entire time period of interest (1969-2006) and an average of more than eight opinions published annually. The volume of such opinions continued to increase dramatically over the course of the current era. such that the average number of opinions published annually tripled from the first half of the period to the second. Further, the total number of prison rape-related decisions published nearly doubled in *each* of the final three years of the contemporary period.[3]

At a historical moment characterized by a highly punitive social mood, a political climate in which law-and-order rhetoric was de rigueur, and a Supreme Court intent on retrenchment of many previously adjudicated prison reforms, the marked increase in cases related to prison rape in the courts seems puzzling at first glance. No doubt a number of factors contribute to a full explanation for this otherwise counter-intuitive phenomenon, including the lobbying and consciousness-raising efforts of various human rights organizations, Justice Blackmun's majority opinion in the landmark prison rape-related case of *Farmer v. Brennan* (1994), and much later, passage of the Prison Rape Elimination Act in 2003. Arguably the most important force driving the increase in prison rape-related cases in the contemporary courts, however, was lawmakers' reconstitution of staff-on-prisoner sexual misconduct as a criminal offense.

According to the American Correctional Association, sexual misconduct "includes, but is not limited to, committing or attempting to commit acts such as sexual assault, sexual abuse, sexual harassment, sexual contact, obscenity, unreasonable and unnecessary invasion of privacy, behavior of a sexual nature or implication, and conversations or correspondence suggesting a romantic or sexual relationship. Sexual misconduct may involve individuals of either sex and may involve interactions between staff and inmates of the same sex."[4] While such behaviors had earlier occurred largely with impunity, during the first four-to-five years of this period the U.S. Congress and more than half of the states' legislatures passed laws defining sexual misconduct by correctional staff as a criminal offense.

The criminalization of staff-on-inmate sexual contact generated a plethora of related cases in the criminal courts, along with a marked increase in individual and class action civil suits based on allegations of sexual misconduct filed against various individuals and departments of corrections.[5] In contrast to the historic period when only one of the 47 opinions published pertained to sexual assault perpetrated by a correctional officer, legal actions related to staff sexual misconduct comprise 64% of the 122 cases related to prison rape published between 1992 and 2006. In the absence of these cases, the dramatic increase in the actual number of prison rape-related opinions published in the contemporary era relative to the historical period would virtually disappear.

DIAGNOSING THE PROBLEM

Rights

The increased volume of prison rape-related litigation in the contemporary-era courts was coincident with a discernable shift in how the subject was framed. In contrast to the very few historical-era cases that had framed prison rape as a rights-related problem, a vast majority of the appellate-level opinions published after 1991 framed sexual violence in prisons first and foremost as a rights issue – specifically a constitutional rights issue. Indeed, more than 81% of the opinions published between 1992 and 2006 employed a rights-related "master frame" in discussing prison rape.

Framed principally as a rights issue, the meaning of prison rape was intimately linked to and, to some extent circumscribed by, the evolving complexities of Eighth Amendment jurisprudence. To recapitulate the evolution of the courts' interpretation of "cruel and unusual punishment" is, on one hand, outside the purview of the current research. At the same time, constituted as a rights issue, the meaning of prison rape is so closely linked to the courts' interpretation of the Amendment's four-word phrase that it is difficult to discuss one without discussing the other. Thus, the section that follows offers a brief, descriptive overview of the emergent meaning of "cruel and unusual punishment," particularly as it pertains to the adjudication of prison rape-related cases.

Descriptive Overview

After more than a hundred years during which legal inquiry into the meaning of the four-word phrase remained dormant – the courts began to flesh out the meaning of "cruel and unusual punishment" under the Eighth Amendment in the late 19th century (Giller 2004).[6] Pertinent to the analysis that follows, in the 1947 U.S. Supreme Court decision in *Louisiana ex rel. Francis v. Resweber*,[7] "intent" became a part of the discussion, paving the way for "the deliberate indifference dilemma" that has continued to occupy the attention of the courts in the contemporary era (Giller 2004: 666). Specifically, in *Resweber*, the Court ruled that harm inflicted on a prisoner by "unforeseeable accident" does not constitute a violation of the Eighth Amendment because it is not intended by the State as an additional penalty to legally valid punishment imposed by the court. Thus, while prisoners may suffer conditions that are cruel and unusual, in the eyes of the Court, if unintended, such harms do not constitute punishment and thus are not actionable under the Eighth Amendment ban.

Almost 30 years later, the Supreme Court's 1976 ruling in *Estelle v. Gamble* established an *objective harm* standard by which future Eighth Amendment claims would be judged. Here, the Court held that only those harms judged "sufficiently serious" as to offend the "evolving standards of decency that mark the progress of a maturing society" could violate the Eighth Amendment. [8] Some years later, in *Wilson v. Seiter* (1991), the Court held that Eighth Amendment claims based on conditions of confinement must be more than just objectively sufficiently serious. To determine the validity of such claims, the court opined, also requires an "inquiry into a prison official's state of mind when it is claimed that the official has inflicted cruel and unusual punishment." [9] Thus, in *Wilson,* the Court expanded the parameters of the deliberate indifference requirement, adding a subjective component to the showing of objective harm needed to establish a viable claim. Based on its 1947 assertion in *Resweber* that intent is implicit in "punishment," for purposes of Eighth Amendment claims based on conditions of confinement, the Court effectively subdivided "deliberate indifference" into two component parts: an *objective component* relating to the seriousness of the harm and a *subjective component,* relating to the state of mind of prison officials. In the absence of a "sufficiently culpable" state of mind, failure to protect an inmate from harm cannot be understood as "punishment" – and therefore, by definition, fails to constitute a viable claim based on the Eighth Amendment.

The Supreme Court's opinion in *Farmer v. Brennan* (1994) set the standard that today remains the benchmark for assessing the validity of Eighth Amendment claims relating to conditions of confinement in general, and prison rape (and other forms of carceral sexual assault) in particular. The various legal arguments and jurisprudential conundrums that comprise *Farmer v. Brennan* have occupied the attention of courts and legal scholars since the case was decided in 1994. Suffice it to say for present purposes that, in *Farmer*, the Court held that being raped in prison is not part of the penalty prisoners are expected to pay for their transgressions, nor does the sexual abuse of prisoners square with prevailing community standards of moral decency. Accordingly, the harm associated with prison rape, the Court asserted, may indeed be found "objectively, sufficiently serious" to violate the Eighth Amendment ban on cruel and unusual punishments. At the same time, however, the Court's extension of the subjective intent requirement set forth in *Wilson* effectively operates to ignore the harm unless plaintiffs can prove that officials acted with 'deliberate indifference' by both knowing of and disregarding those conditions."[10] In other words, whether or not the risk of harm to an inmate was so obvious that it should have been perceived is not sufficient. To state a viable Eighth Amendment claim, after *Farmer*, prisoners were required to show that defendants actually *did* perceive the risk and, armed with that knowledge, *consciously* chose not to act, or chose to act in a manner that was clearly insufficient to alleviate the potential harm.

Harm

Whether perpetrated by prisoners or correctional staff, in the context of cases employing a "rights" master frame, rape, sexual assault, sexual abuse, and sexual harassment in carceral settings were (necessarily) framed as "harm." The measure, meaning, and consequences of specific manifestations of such harm were argued, defined, and delineated in an ongoing discourse about "cruel and unusual punishment" in the courts throughout the contemporary era. Although a "harm frame" was universally deployed in rights-based cases, the data revealed notable variations in the characterization of sexual violence in prison in terms of "harm." Indeed, analysis of these data indicated that cases deploying a "prisoner-on-prisoner assault" script differed markedly from cases deploying a "sexual misconduct" script in terms of the nature and extent of the harm constituted by each.

Harm and Prisoner-On-Prisoner Violence

Among the opinions that that framed prison rape as "harm," about 20% deployed a "prisoner-on-prisoner violence" script. In these cases, rape, sexual assault, and sexual abuse in carceral settings were overwhelmingly represented in terms of violence and, accordingly, were discussed in a vocabulary aimed at depicting physical brutality and its attendant corporal, psychological, and spiritual consequences.

Discourse deploying a prisoner-on-prisoner rape script commonly included descriptions of bloody struggles, screaming victims, multiple-perpetrator "gang rapes," powerful predators, and/or ongoing brutality and terrorism that left their marks unmistakably inscribed on the bodies and psyches of victims. In *Little v. Shelby County* (2000), for example, the plaintiff claimed to have been raped by several members of a prison gang. Testimony in the case included descriptions of violent sexual assaults perpetrated by members of both the Vice Lords and Gangster Disciples, two gangs that reportedly "controlled the activities of the inmates in the pods in roughly 95% of the [Shelby County] Jail."[11] Rapes and other sexual assaults perpetrated by members of these gangs were carried out in the context of brutal physical attacks and punishments known as "Thunderdomes," which occurred out of sight of correctional staff and commonly lasted all night long. In addition to the sexual assaults, the violence that constituted a "Thunderdome" generally included kicking, punching, and hog-tying of non-gang-member prisoners, one of whom was allegedly lassoed with a rope around his neck, hogtied, and beaten until his jaw was broken, "before a guard heard him screaming and ordered the [gang members] to release him."[12]

In *Pulliam v. Shelby County* (2005), the plaintiff, a pre-trial detainee, was placed in a cell with two-to-four convicted felons, who were awaiting transport to maximum-security facilities. Several days thereafter, Pulliam was raped and severely beaten by some number of his pod-mates. A description of the assault itself is absent from the opinion in the case. However, a litany of Pulliam's resulting physical injuries and hardships is indicative of the extent to which the rape is understood in terms of the violence that accompanied it.

> A physician testified that the plaintiff would have a lifelong disability. Plaintiff is no longer able to run or participate in sports that he previously enjoyed, like ice skating or water skiing. He walks with a limp and is required to wear a TENS unit to control the pain.[13] He has had a total hip replacement, suffered broken ribs and a broken wrist, endured the pain of the injuries, suffering, surgery and had to learn to walk again. His broken wrist bones have deprived him of his livelihood and enjoyment of his hobbies. Plaintiff continues to have blurred vision as well as a significant hearing loss, and has

experienced significant psychological trauma. Plaintiff also testified that he has nightmares and paranoia, and that the trauma resulting from the attempted rape deprived him of his ability to have intimate physical relations for several years. He continues to have body memory experiences where his face swells and he experiences physical pain again.[14]

Only slightly less brutal than the events in *Little* (2000) and *Pulliam* (2005), the depiction of the assault scenario in *Kemner v. Hemphill* (2002) is perhaps more typical of those constituting prison rape in terms of physical violence. In Kemner, the plaintiff alleged that he had been beaten extensively over a two-hour period and ultimately was forced to perform oral sex on his much larger and more powerful cellmate. Kemner "'suffered physical pain, cuts, scrapes, and bruises' as well as 'mental anguish, fright, and shock, embarrassment, humiliation and mortification, in addition to psychological injuries that are permanent.'"[15] He further claimed that he had vomited after his attacker ejaculated in his mouth. As the court noted in its opinion:

> Plaintiff here alleges physical injury which is more than *de minimis*. He alleges that he was assaulted for two hours, suffered cuts, bruises and abrasions, and he was so physically ill that he vomited. He alleges that a witness would testify that he was in shock for hours afterwards. Any physical force which causes the human body to convulse in vomiting and to go into shock has caused physical injury...[16]

In a number of cases, violence – or the potential for violence – was implicit in perpetrators' number, physical size, race, and/or history of aggressive behavior relative to their diminutive, non-violent, naïve victims. In *Wilson v. Wright, et al.* (1998),[17] for example, plaintiff Wilson, an 18-year-old, 5'8" tall, 136 pound inmate brought a § 1983 action stemming from his rape by Robert Ramey, a 38-year-old, 6'1", 290 pound African American. Seven days after he was assigned to Ramey's cell, Ramey assaulted and sodomized Wilson. As the court noted:

> A review of Ramey's file would have been quite illuminating. It would have disclosed a scoring sheet that marked him as an

inmate with a high propensity for violence....Specifically, the file indicated acts of inflicting bodily injury on a prison guard, maliciously injuring a correctional employee, damaging property for the purpose of rendering the prison facility less secure, threatening and assaulting correctional officers, unauthorized presence in another inmate's cell for the purpose of covert sexual activities, disobeying direct orders, assaulting other inmates, sexual assault of a young woman, and sexual assault of a fellow inmate in the county jail. Moreover, only three months prior to plaintiff's transfer to Greensville, inmate Ramey was convicted of assaulting another inmate.[18]

The court continued:

Ramey, a six-foot-one-inch, 290-pound Black inmate with a history of prison assaults and a high-security classification, was imprisoned for raping a small, young, white male. Plaintiff, a small, young, white male, had a low-security classification, was in prison for a nonviolent offense, and feared sexual attack because of his size and other physical characteristics. Based on these undisputed facts, a jury could well find that Ramey posed a risk of serious harm to his cellmate.[19]

Justice Blackmun's opinion in *Farmer v. Brennan* (1994) perhaps best sums up the discourse about prisoner-on-prisoner rape in the contemporary era. Blackmun's opinion has been cited, dissected, discussed, parsed, and analyzed extensively and repeatedly within the legal community and elsewhere since its publication in 1994. It would be difficult to overstate the frequency with which later courts, legal scholars, social scientists, policy makers and others have cited Blackmun's now-iconic discourse on the subject. In *Farmer* (1994), Justice Blackman spoke of prison rape in almost exclusively in terms of violence and its attendant corporal, psychological, and spiritual harms that resulted from it:

The horrors experienced by many young inmates, particularly those who, like petitioner, are convicted of nonviolent offenses, border on the unimaginable. Prison rape not only threatens the lives of those who fall prey to their aggressors, but is potentially devastating to the human spirit. Shame, depression, and a shattering loss of self-esteem accompany the perpetual terror the victim thereafter must endure....Unable to fend for himself and without the protection of prison officials, the victim finds himself at the mercy of larger, stronger, and ruthless inmates. Although formally sentenced to a term of incarceration, many inmates discover that their punishment, even for nonviolent offenses like credit card fraud or tax evasion, degenerates into a reign of terror....[20]

As the cases discussed above suggest, framed as a rights issue, prisoner-on-prisoner rape was constituted and understood in the contemporary era as violence. Indeed, in the context of Eighth Amendment claims – and circumscribed by requirement of physical harm placed on prisoner-generated litigation by the PLRA (1996) – the courts were largely incapable of understanding prisoner-on-prisoner rape in terms other than violence and, evidently, its attendant physical, psychological and spiritual consequences.

Harm and Sexual Misconduct

While only one historical-era opinion had pertained to staff-on-prisoner sexual misconduct, in the contemporary-era cases deploying a sexual misconduct script constituted the modal category. About 80% of contemporary opinions framing prison rape primarily as harm drew on this script. Concomitant with the glut of cases related to staff-on-prisoner sexual abuse after 1991 was an equally dramatic increase in the number of opinions related to claims involving female prisoners – specifically, female prisoners who were victims of staff sexual misconduct. While only one appellate opinion published during the historical era pertained to female victims,[21] in the contemporary era, more than 40% of cases deploying a sexual misconduct script involved female victims.

Like the opinions discussed in the preceding section, cases relying on a sexual misconduct script focused on an array of incidents ranging from sexual harassment to sexual abuse to sexual battery to rape. In sharp contrast to the representation of prisoner-on-prisoner incidents, however, the discourse generated in cases of sexual misconduct constituted the harm inherent in these events in entirely different terms. While all manner of prisoner-on-prisoner assaults were constituted as "violence" measured and understood entirely in terms of their gruesome corporal manifestations, sexual misconduct – as the term, in fact, implies – was understood in terms that rendered such incidents not so much about violence as about illicit sex, perverse sensuality, and abuse of power.

In cases relying on a sexual misconduct script, sexually-charged incidents often occurred in the context of – and sometimes were not easy to distinguish from – "day-to-day operations" or "standard procedures" that characterized the carceral environment. In *Buckley v. Dallas County, et al.* (2000),[22] for example, the plaintiff brought a § 1983 civil rights action, alleging that prison guards sexually assaulted him by "fondling his genitals" during a routine pat-down search. It is important to note that Buckley claimed neither that the scope of, nor the justification for, the search was unreasonable but instead alleged that individual prison guards acting of their own accord used the opportunity afforded by a pat-down search to sexually molest him. According to the plaintiff, the "prison guards fondled him in an inappropriate manner while conducting a routine pat-down search and only stopped because he did not become excited."[23]

Similarly, in *Webb v. Forman* (1996), it was asserted that:

> During the course of a pat frisk, conducted while he was standing up against a wall, Officer Forman [sic] put his hands down Webb's pants. Webb alleges that Officer Forman moved his hands down to Webb's penis, fondled his penis with his fingers, and grabbed his genitals. Webb further alleges that while Officer Forman's hands were down his pants, Officer Forman "caressed" him.

> Webb alleges that Forman's hands were down his pants for " a few seconds." Webb alleges that when he confronted Officer Forman about this alleged foundling [sic], grabbing, and caressing, he was ordered to stand back on the wall. Webb states that he once again stood against the wall, and Officer Forman conducted a second pat frisk. Webb further alleges that Officer Forman once again went to place his hands under Webb's shirt. Webb states that in anticipation of Officer

Forman once again putting his hands down his pants, Webb broke away from Officer Forman. Webb states that Officer Forman performed a third pat frisk on him, but this was a routine pat frisk because a sergeant had arrived and was standing right next to Webb.[24]

Likewise, in yet another case, *Rodriguez v. McClenning* (2005) the plaintiff alleged that an officer used the opportunity afforded by an otherwise legitimate procedure to sexually molest him:

As [he] waited in line to go out to the yard for evening recreation, he was selected for a pat-frisk. Officer McClenning told Rodriguez that he was being frisked because McClenning had received information that Rodriguez brought contraband into the yard the previous day. McClenning directed Rodriguez to assume a pat-frisk position against the wall. After Rodriguez complied with this demand, however, McClenning put on unauthorized black leather gloves (instead of the latex gloves usually used for pat-frisks) and started punching his fists together in an intimidating manner. McClenning then told Rodriguez to keep his arms and legs stretched out and if Rodriguez felt "[McClenning's] hands in [Rodriguez's] ass...don't think about screaming because no one is going to help." McClenning then conducted the pat-frisk in an inappropriate manner than included caressing Rodriguez's chest and repeatedly groping his genitals and buttocks.[25]

In the case of *Bromell v. Idaho Department of Corrections* (2006), the plaintiff alleged similar abuses by a correctional officer:

On August 16, 2005, Steven Bromell was inappropriately fondled ...by Defendant Officer Kyle while returning from the prison recreation yard at the Idaho State Correction Institution at Orofino, Idaho. At that time and place, Defendant Officer Kyle approached Mr. Bromell from behind and placed his penis against Mr. Bromell's buttocks without Mr. Bromell's consent. Defendant Officer Kyle then reached around to Mr. Bromell's chest and squeezed his pectoral muscles. Defendant

Officer Kyle then ran his hands down to Mr. Bromell's penis, squeezed his genitals, and said, "You fuckin' inmates must like this shit if you're in here. Do you like it when I do this?"[26]

In *Evans and Jordan v. City of Zebulon, Loomis and Stephens* (2003), two pre-trial detainees sued the City of Zebulon, Georgia and relevant officers of the city's police force based on allegations that they experienced sexual abuse while being searched prior to booking on charges of speeding, driving while intoxicated, and parole violation. In the context of those proceedings, Officer Stephens allegedly took plaintiff Jordan into a utility closet, patted him down and then ordered him to remove his shoes and shirt. He then ordered Jordan to lower his pants. At this point another officer pushed Evans into the room, causing him to stumble into Jordan, and both men fell to the ground. The officers picked the men up and pushed them back against the wall. Stephens then pulled Jordan's underwear down and placed a slender black object between Jordan's buttocks, jabbing his anus. Startled, Jordan jumped, causing the two officers to "laugh and giggle."[27] Stephens ordered Jordan to use his hands to spread his buttocks. Stephens repeated these actions on Evans, placing the object between his buttocks, then used it to lift each man's genitals. Stephens was alleged to have made racially derogatory remarks and, while using the slender metal object on the two men, referred to prison rape.

Similar scenarios were depicted in *Young v. Poff* (2006), *Nelson v. Michalko* (1999), and *Styles v. McGinnis* (2001). In the former, the plaintiff alleged "a single incident of sexual assault, being groped by one of the two corrections officers during a single pat frisk."[28] In *Nelson* (1999), the plaintiff claimed that Correctional Officer Michalko "intentionally...shoved the hand held metal detector up inside my anal body area for no reason, sexually assaulting me with it."[29] Finally, in, *Styles v. McGinnis* (2001), prisoner Timothy W. Styles filed a § 1983 claim, alleging a conspiracy among two prison guards and an emergency room employee to molest him during the course of a medical examination in violation of his Eighth Amendment rights.[30]

Male prisoners were by no means the only ones who were alleged to have experienced sexual molestation in the context of what might otherwise have constituted "standard procedures" in correctional institutions. As the case of *Jordan et al. v. Gardner et al.* (1993)

suggests, however, in the case of female inmates, it is difficult to ascertain when the sexual component of molestation was intentional and when it was simply inherent in the procedure itself. In *Jordan* (1993), multiple plaintiffs instituted a civil rights action after policy was implemented allowing male guards to conduct random, non-emergency body searches of female inmates. Several of the inmates allegedly were either molested during the course of these cross-gender body searches or experienced these "reasonable" searches as molestation, suffering severe emotional distress in their wake. In 1992, The *Jordan* plaintiffs filed a claim alleging that cross-gender body searches violated their Eighth Amendment rights.[31]

The court record in *Jordan* contains an account of the specific activities that comprise a "clothed body search," as well as its alleged impact on one particular plaintiff:

> During the cross-gender clothed body search, the male guard stands next to the female inmate and thoroughly runs his hands over her clothed body starting with her neck and working down to her feet. According to the prison training material, a guard is to "use a flat hand and pushing motion across the inmate's crotch area." The guard must "push inward and upward when searching the crotch and upper thighs of the inmate." All seams in the leg and the crotch area are to be "squeezed and kneaded." Using the back of the hand, the guard also is to search the breast area in a sweeping motion, so that the breasts will be "flattened."...A training film, viewed by the court, gave the impression that a thorough search would last several minutes.

> Several inmates were searched by male guards on the first day of implementation. One unwillingly submitted to...[the]search and suffered severe distress: she had to have her fingers pried loose from the bars she had grabbed during the search, and she vomited after returning to her cell block.[32]

The data are replete with accounts of correctional staff members who abused their position of power, turning otherwise standard procedures and routine operations into sexualized events for their own entertainment and/or gratification. The various examples described above by no means exhaust this very large volume of discourse. They are, however, thoroughly representative of it. Indeed, what is remarkable about this discourse is its sameness – that, and the extent to which it stands in sharp contrast to the discourse generated in cases of prisoner-on-prisoner assault. While violence is arguably implicit in staff-on-prisoner sexual abuse, as well as in abuse of power in general, the discourse about staff-on-prisoner sexual abuse represented these incidents in relatively non-violent terms. The "groping," "pressing," "kneading," "fondling," and "caressing" that characterized these highly sexualized illicit behaviors are remarkable in contrast to the brutality and mayhem that constituted prisoner-on-prisoner incidents.

The discourse about sexual abuse in the context of "standard procedures," while extensive, does not tell the whole story. In addition to the sexual scenarios described above, a whole array of alleged abuses occurred outside the parameters of routine operations. Indeed, the discourse about correctional officers and other staff who sought perverse pleasures and sexual gratification at the expense of prisoners, and did so without relying on the "cover" afforded by otherwise legitimate procedures, is abundant. As the examples to follow will indicate, the discourse around this latter type of incident again relied heavily on a vocabulary of sex and sexuality, in contrast to the lexicon of violence that characterized the discourse about prisoner-on-prisoner incidents.

In *Boddie v. Schneider, et al.* (1997), for example, the plaintiff alleged that one of the defendants "made a pass at him." "Schneider [allegedly] squeezed his hand, touched his penis, and said 'You know your [sic] a sexy black devil, I like you.'"[33] Some weeks after the first sexual overture, Boddie asserted, the officer stopped him, "'bumping into [his] chest with both her breasts so hard [he] could feel the points of her nipples against [his] chest.' Boddie states that Schneider did this to Boddie twice, pinning him to a door. When he tried to pass her again, Schneider again bumped into him, this time 'with her whole body, vagina against penis, pinning [him] to the door.'"[34]

In a similar case, *White v. Ottinger, et al* (2006), another female correctional officer with an alleged history of molesting young male inmates was accused by the plaintiff of sexual abuse. White claimed:

> [Officer Mayfield] flirted with him, and then wrote provocative letters to him, ultimately as many as fifteen to

twenty. At some time after she wrote the first letter, Mayfield sexually assaulted White by rubbing her body against his, grabbing and touching his body, and forcibly performing oral sex [on him]. Thereafter, Mayfield performed oral sex on White on four or five occasions. White testified that, although he found 'the act of oral sex itself' to be 'pleasurable,' he felt that he had no choice in the matter. He was afraid that, if he did not cooperate, Mayfield would retaliate by making him lose his job at the commissary, accusing him of prison misconduct, inflicting disciplinary action, and/or delaying his parole.[35]

In *Doe v. Scroggy et al.* (2006), the plaintiff alleged:

[He] noticed [male Correctional Officer] Tuft observing him in the shower, and was fairly certain that Tuft winked at him. When Plaintiff got out of the shower, he put on a pair of shorts and went to the laundry room to get additional clothing. While Plaintiff was in the laundry room, Tuft approached him from behind, reached around him, and grabbed his penis....Following the laundry room incident, Tuft continued his sexual advances towards Plaintiff by writing a series of sexually suggestive notes to him and leaving them in his bunk or in his locker. While Tuft made Plaintiff return three of the notes, Plaintiff kept a fourth note, which read: "J, I want you so damn bad it doesn't even make since [sic]. I know you might not believe this, but I think about you constantly and I wanna be with you, I won't stop until I get you. W/B soon. Why you so damn fine??"

Sometime in the late afternoon on or about August 2, 2002, Tuft directed Plaintiff to follow him to a room located adjacent to the "big TV room" in Holly A Hall. When the two entered the room, Tuft showed Plaintiff his penis and began masturbating. While this was occurring, Tuft reached over and touched Plaintiff's penis, over Plaintiff's shorts. When Tuft finished, he ejaculated on the front of Plaintiff's t-shirt and told Plaintiff to clean it up. During the incident, Tuft told Plaintiff not to tell anyone about their encounter, or he would claim that Plaintiff assaulted him and Plaintiff would "spend the rest of [his] life in prison."

That same day, after 9:00 p.m., Tuft came to Plaintiff's bunk and told Plaintiff to follow him. Tuft led Plaintiff to the back porch area of Holly A Hall and told Plaintiff to sit down. Tuft then pulled his penis out of his pants and ordered Plaintiff to perform oral sex on him. When Plaintiff hesitated, Tuft again threatened to report Plaintiff for assault, then grabbed Plaintiff's head and forced him to comply with his request. When Plaintiff finished, Tuft ejaculated in Plaintiff's mouth and on Plaintiff's t-shirt.[36]

Clearly violence was implicit in the discourse described above and coercion explicit. At the same time, when contrasted with prisoner-on-prisoner scenarios, these incidents were depicted in terms that were remarkably non-violent. Indeed – bizarre as it may seem – they contain elements commonly associated with romantic relationships. Specifically, these included flirting, the giving of compliments (however unwelcome), the exchange of "provocative" notes, the experience of sexual "pleasure." In the two examples that follow, a number of these same elements were present, along with the giving of "gifts" (in the form of lingerie, candy, and drugs), "caressing," "hugging," and "kissing." In *Cain v. Rock and Anne Arundel County* (1999) the court record contained the following allegations:

[Plaintiff's cellmate, Reed,] told a Detention Center supervisor that on March 16 or 17 Rock had visited the cell that Cain shared with Reed. While Reed pretended to sleep, she observed Rock give Cain a number of gifts, including bras, thong underwear, cigarettes, candy, and yellow pills. According to Reed, Rock asked Cain to model the underwear and then engaged Cain in an act of cunnilingus. Reed also stated that Cain told her that she and Rock had engaged in "sex" a "number of times in that cell."

On March 21, Detention Center officials advised Rock that he had been placed on administrative leave pending investigation into the matter. That evening, Detention Center officers conducted a "shake down" of Cain's cell and recovered the contraband items detailed above. When officials questioned Cain, she stated that Rock had given her the items, but they had only "hugged and kissed."

Four days later, the County Police interviewed a second inmate, Brenda Fitzsimmons, who had occupied a cell adjacent to Cain's cell. Fitzsimmons told the investigator that on three occasions during March 1997 she observed Rock entering Cain's cell and heard sounds she associated with sexual activity. Fitzsimmons also claimed that Cain had told her that she had been a willing participant in the sexual activity, but was going to charge Rock with rape and "take him for everything he's got."

The Police interviewed Cain the following day. She stated that Rock had given her gifts on different occasions and the two had started kissing and writing notes. Cain also stated that their interaction had culminated in a single act of intercourse. When asked if Rock had ever forced or threatened her in order to obtain sex, Cain answered that "he did sort of lead me, but he didn't force me." In the pleadings and discovery, Cain has alleged that, during the time of the incidents, she was in a "psychotic state of mind" due to various medications. She has also stated that Rock's gifts to her resulted in infractions that kept her under Rock's supervision. Finally, Cain has also alleged that Rock took advantage of her mental and physical state to engage in non-consensual sexual acts with her.[37]

Similarly, in *Szydlowski et al. v. Ohio Department of Rehabilitation and Correction* (1992) plaintiff female inmates claimed that an aide who had been hired to provide psychological counseling services had sexually abused them. Sydlowski testified that the psychological aide had provided her with contraband items, "kissed her, hugged her, and caused her to perform fellatio on him."[38] A second plaintiff in the case, Ms. Gould, alleged that the aide "kissed her, hugged her, caressed her, and attempted to have intercourse with her."[39] Other parties to the case made similar allegations regarding sexual abuse by the psychological aide.

In another case involving the giving of "gifts," or more accurately "bribes," the sexual abuse of a transgender prisoner occupied the attention of the court. In *Schwenk v. Hartford* (2000), however, the depiction of alleged events are representative of a number of more violent and coercive staff-on-prisoner assaults. Schwenk, a transgender plaintiff alleged:

Shortly after she arrived in Baker Unit, Mitchell subjected her to an escalating series of unwelcome sexual advances and harassment that culminated in a sexual assault. This harassment began with "winking, performing explicit actions imitating oral sex, making obscene comments, watching Plaintiff in the shower while 'grinding' his hand on his crotch area, and repeatedly demanding that Plaintiff engage in sexual acts with him." Then, in late 1994, Mitchell asked Schwenk to have sex with him in the staff bathroom, offering to bring her make-up and "girl stuff" in exchange for sex. When she refused and attempted to walk away, Mitchell grabbed her and groped her buttocks. Schwenk pushed him away and ran back to her cell crying.

Later that day, Mitchell again approached Schwenk and told her that he had had oral sex with a former inmate and planned to have sex with his neighbor's young son, who he claimed to be "grooming" for the experience. Shortly thereafter, Schwenk says that Mitchell entered her cell, saw that they were alone, and demanded that Schwenk perform oral sex on him. Schwenk refused and told him to get out. Mitchell then turned and looked behind him to make sure no one was coming, unzipped his pants, pulled out his penis, and again demanded that Schwenk perform oral sex. She again rebuffed him and again told him to leave. Although Mitchell said he would leave, he did not. Instead, according to Schwenk, Mitchell closed the door to her cell, grabbed her, turned her around, pushed her against the bars, and began grinding his exposed penis into her buttocks. Schwenk testified that...Mitchell ignored her struggling and continued to rub his penis against her, saying "oh baby, I knew you'd be good." Apparently fearing detection, Mitchell abruptly pushed away from Schwenk, zipped up his pants, and left hastily.[40]

Among the cases that framed sexual assault in prisons as a rights issue, those deploying a sexual misconduct script offer a seemingly endless supply of graphic examples similar to those offered above. The point, however, is not to overwhelm the reader with examples which become undeniably repetitive and, arguably, gratuitous. Rather, the goal here is to render visible the nature of the discourse about staff-on-prisoner sexual misconduct and to highlight the rather remarkable contrast between this discourse and the representation of prisoner-on-prisoner violence discussed in the preceding section.

Despite the fact that the parameters of Eighth Amendment jurisprudence and the showing of physical harm required by the PLRA were equally imposed on cases of prisoner-on-prisoner sexual assault and cases of sexual misconduct, the two types of sexual violence were construed quite differently. Indeed, as the examples provided illustrate, prisoner-on-prisoner assault was understood almost entirely as violence measured by the extent of corporal harm resulting from it, while incidents of staff-on-prisoner misconduct were discussed in terms that rendered them highly sexualized, sometimes quasi-romantic, coercive – albeit non-violent abuses of power perpetrated by officers and other staff unable to contain their lust for the inmates in their charge.

ATTRIBUTING BLAME

As indicated earlier in this chapter, among the appellate opinions that comprise the data for this portion of the analysis, those framing the problem of prison rape primarily as a rights issue comprised the modal category. Regardless of the script deployed or the severity of the sexual violence alleged, the *legal* attribution of blame in these cases turned on the subjective element of the two-part test set forth in *Farmer v. Brennan*. Once a plaintiff's allegations were judged "sufficiently serious" – and for the most part they were – the court turned to the question of "intent," which at its core, amounted to culpability or "blame." Intent was understood to be implied in an officer's action (or inaction) when it was shown that s/he knew, or should have known, of a risk of serious harm to a prisoner and consciously disregarded it (as evidenced, for example, by: 1) his/her failure to take steps aimed at abating a perceived risk of sexual violence; or 2) his/her perpetration of sexual violence). In the presence of deliberate indifference, "serious harm" was legally reconstituted as "cruel and unusual punishment." Conversely, where intent was absent, sexual victimization simply became an unfortunate but not unconstitutional condition of confinement.

Having said this, it should it should be noted that the courts were by no means blind to the broader world beyond the restrictive environment of Eighth Amendment jurisprudence. Clearly, the they did not condone the sexual victimization of prisoners by one another nor by correctional personnel and, notwithstanding the legal outcome of a given case, frequently expressed their abhorrence of carceral sexual violence as well as sympathy for its victims. In more than one instance when a prisoner's allegation of sexual victimization lacked viability as a constitutional matter, the court's opinion nevertheless included "suggestions" that the plaintiff's allegations might nevertheless amount to a civil tort under state law, or at least cause for internal disciplinary action against an offending correctional officer.

Blaming Prisoners

While a number of contemporary era opinions discussed "homosexuals" in the role of victims, the "violent homosexual rapist" had apparently ceased to be the iconic sexual boogie man of the cell block. Indeed, the conflation of violence and homosexuality that had been culturally pervasive in earlier decades had, by the 1990s, been replaced by the representation of homosexual prisoners as non-agentive, hyper-vulnerable, and often effeminate. Along with the increasing "normalization" of homosexuality outside prison walls, the reconstitution of gay prisoners as the carceral "weaker sex" essentially rendered the violent homosexual prison rapist a cultural contradiction.

Likewise, while "race" looms large in social science, correctional, and popular discourse about prison rape in the contemporary era, it was only rarely appeared in appellate opinions published after 1991. On the few occasions when race was mentioned in a contemporary-era opinion, it was included among number of "characteristics" collectively intended to represent either "power and dangerousness" or, in the case of whites, "vulnerability." The court's opinion in *Wilson v. Wright, et al.* (1998) (cited earlier in this chapter) offers examples of this deployment of race:

> In addressing defendant's summary judgment motion, the initial question under Farmer is whether plaintiff was exposed to an objectively substantial risk of harm. Given the instant facts, a jury could find such a risk existed. Ramey, a six-foot-one-inch, 290-pound Black inmate with a history of prison assaults and a high-security classification, was imprisoned for raping a small, young, white male. Plaintiff, a small, young, white male, had a low-security classification, was in prison for a nonviolent offense, and feared sexual attack because of his size and other physical characteristics. Based on these undisputed facts, a jury could well find that Ramey posed a risk of serious harm to his cellmate.[41]

Despite the fact that race was occasionally conflated with power, vulnerability, and/or risk as it was in *Wilson v. Wright* (1998), analysis of the data indicated that race did not play an overt role in contemporary era legal discourse about prison rape. Indeed, by the contemporary era, prisoners in general had largely ceased to be blamed for the problem of prison rape. While "types" of prisoners had historically been identified as perpetrators and, accordingly, blamed for the problem of epidemic sexual violence plaguing U.S. prisons, contemporary era appellate opinions contained little evidence that any specific group of prisoners was blamed for the problem – even the "violent type" that perpetrated acts of sexual terrorism. Indeed, construed as violence, prisoner-on-prisoner rape appears, by this time, to have become just another *part* of the pervasive risk of carceral violence that correctional personnel were charged with managing.

Blaming Correctional Officers

Overwhelmingly, the scripts deployed in appellate-level opinions in the contemporary era blamed individual correctional officers for the problem of prison rape. Regardless of the outcome of the cases before the courts, corrections officers were represented at best as careless in their disregard for prisoners' safety and well being and, at worst, wanton, malevolent, predatory, perverse, and sadistic. Contemporary-era opinions are replete with allegations that officers tolerated, facilitated, perpetrated, encouraged, laughed at and/or ignored sexual violence within the institutions that employed them. Although the rare officer who intervened to prevent or interrupt the victimization of prisoners was not entirely absent from the discourse, such references were anomalies, certainly not the rule.

Prisoner-on-Prisoner Assault

In contemporary-era appellate opinions, cases deploying a prisoner-on-prisoner rape script commonly included graphic details of brutal abuse and prolonged sexual torture along with what at least appear to be highly credible allegations that officers knew of the violence, or at least the risk of violence, taking place under their noses but, at the same time, did not choose to intervene. In light of this, the extent of the debate over the attribution of legal blame in these cases is somewhat surprising. Indeed, even at the appellate level, it was not uncommon for courts to find that prisoners failed even to establish a question of material fact in regard to officers' culpability under the Eighth Amendment. Thus, as the following examples suggest, there was often a marked disjuncture between the discursive and legal attributions of blame for prisoner-on-prisoner sexual assaults..

In *Webb v. Lawrence County* (1998),[42] the plaintiff, who at the time was 19 years old, about 5'4" tall and weighed about120 pounds, was assigned to share a cell with Greg Wyman, a maximum security inmate convicted of multiple sex offenses – specifically, rape and forcible sodomy on a male minor. Webb alleged that Wyman sexually assaulted him repeatedly over the course of a four-day period. Because Wyman had a knife, which the plaintiff feared might be used to retaliate against him if he "snitched," he told no one about his situation. Subsequently, while Wyman was in the shower, Webb managed to smuggle a note to officers informing them of his situation. Ultimately, he filed a civil rights action in federal district court alleging that various officers on duty violated his constitutional rights. Among other things, he alleged that defendants acted with reckless disregard for his constitutional rights by failing to protect him from sexual assault when they placed him in the cell of a known sexual predator despite his obvious vulnerability to such assault.

Similarly, in *Young v. Quinlan et al.* (1992), the plaintiff alleged
that his Eighth Amendment rights were violated when officials at the
United States Penitentiary at Lewisburg, Pennsylvania failed to protect
him from sexual attacks by other inmates. According to the facts in the
case:

> During the late night and early morning hours of April 21-22,
> Young's violent ordeal at Lewisburg began. Young's cellmate
> began asking Young, repeatedly, to have sex with him. After
> Young refused, his cellmate threatened Young and attempted
> to climb on his bunk. At one point an officer making his
> rounds approached the cell. Young's cellmate told Young that
> if he said anything to the officer he would be killed. After the
> officer left, Young's cellmate "started slapping [him]
> demanding sex." Young was able to ward off his cellmate's
> sexual advances that night.

The next morning, Young handed an inmate-orderly a note
addressed to Officer Steven Bilger describing the incident.
Bilger then came to Young's cell and told Young that he could
not be moved....After Bilger left, Young's cellmate began
"spitting in plaintiff's face, slap[ping] him up side his head
and shoving [him] into the wall." An inmate-orderly saw the
incident and alerted Bilger. Bilger again came to Young's cell
and Young again asked to be moved. Bilger then told Young
that he should write a letter asking to be moved and that he
would take it to Lieutenant London. Young's cellmate told
Young that if he wrote anyone a letter he would be killed.
Young wrote the letter and handed it to the inmate-orderly to
give to Bilger. Young was then moved to a new cell.

One week later, Young's new cellmate assaulted him and
demanded sex. Young again warded off his cellmate's sexual
demands. The new cellmate also threatened to kill Young if
he told anyone of the incident. That night, Young wrote a
letter to Lieutenant London and Captain Thomas telling them
of the incident, and requesting protective custody. Prison
officials did nothing. On May 15, Young's cellmate dunked
Young's head in a toilet in an attempt to convince Young to

have sex with him. Young wrote another letter to Keohane, Thomas and London telling them of the incident and again he requested protection. Prison officials again did nothing.[43]

Notwithstanding the fact that the plaintiffs' Eighth Amendment claims in each of these cases failed to survive summary judgment, the depiction of events indicate that discursively, if not constitutionally, blame for the violence was placed at the door of correctional officers involved. Likewise, the case of prisoner, Kendall Spruce, is instructive in this regard. Spruce claimed that he was raped repeatedly over the course of a one-year period, by more than twenty different prisoners, at least one of whom infected him with HIV. At trial, Spruce introduced documents demonstrating that one of the defendants, Officer Sargent, while clearly aware of the series of rapes, denied Spruce's request not to be celled with an inmate who had previously forced Spruce to perform sexual acts against his will. Further, Officer Sargent's own narrative rendered his indifference to Spruce's safety all the more obvious. Indeed, Sargent indicated that he was aware of the fact that inmates at the prison commonly had to fight off sexual aggressors and that it was "the inmates own responsibility to let people understand that they're not going to put up with that." [44]

Interestingly, in contrast to the narrative and evidence that rendered Sargent blameworthy, very similar evidence and a nearly identical narrative concerning the actions of another defendant, Officer Norris, appears to have absolved the officer of at least some portion of blame for his failure to act on Spruce's behalf. Although Spruce produced a document signed by Norris in which the prisoner complained of being forced to cell with inmates who jumped on him and forced him to perform sexual acts against his will, in regard to Norris's culpability, the court remarked that "'an officials' failure to alleviate a significant risk that he should have perceived but did not, while no cause for commendation,' is not deliberate indifference to an inmate's health or safety and therefore not a violation of the Eighth Amendment." [45]

Sexual Misconduct

While contemporary-era perpetrators no longer bore the blame for prisoner-on-prisoner sexual violence, perpetrators of sexual misconduct did not enjoy the same luxury. Indeed, contemporary era cases that framed prisoner rape as harm and deployed a sexual misconduct script generated little if any debate about who was to blame for the problem. Represented as "rogue officers" or "bad apples," officer/perpetrators were clearly represented as the principal bearers of blame for the problem. As the court wrote in *Boddie v. Schneider et al.* (1997):

> Sexual abuse of a prisoner by a corrections officer has no legitimate penological purpose, and is "simply not part of the penalty offenders pay for their offenses against society." Where no legitimate law enforcement or penological purpose can be inferred from the defendant's alleged conduct, the abuse itself may be sufficient evidence of a sufficiently culpable state of mind.[46]

The data are replete with examples in which blame for the problem of staff-on-prisoner sexual misconduct was implicitly or explicitly attributed to a particular type of officer – specifically those "bad apples," who, acting individually or collectively outside the parameters of their professional duties, abused their position(s) of trust and their power over prisoners for their own entertainment or to gratify themselves sexually, or both. Narrative testimony depicting the acts of these miscreant officers offered extensive descriptions of lewd behaviors and appalling abuses recounted in lurid detail. In *Wisconsin v. Terrell* (2006), for example, an officer assigned to transport a female prisoner to a holding cell in a courthouse, instead led her into a small bathroom where he locked the door, removed her handcuffs and belly chains, "then lifted up her shirt and pushed her bra up, exposing her breasts. Terrell then licked and sucked her breasts, pulled down her pants and underwear and then licked her vaginal area. After that, Terrell unzipped his pants, removed his erect penis, and masturbated to ejaculation while rubbing her bare buttocks. Terrell then told [the prisoner] to put her clothes back on" and he replaced her restraints. He then escorted her to the holding cell warning her not to tell anyone about the incident.[47]

Hammond, et al. v. Gordon County et al. (2002) offers another example of staff misconduct so serious that blame is implicit in the depiction of the abuses themselves. In this case, a number of officers were alleged to have required all female prisoners to expose their breasts in order to obtain toilet paper, feminine hygiene products, and other basic necessities. Additionally prisoners in one officer's charge were required to fellate the officer or perform oral sex on one another while he watched in order to obtain permission to use the bathroom. Those who refused to cooperate had no choice but to urinate or defecate on themselves. Incredibly, the allegations of abuse in the 40-page opinion escalated far beyond those just discussed and included, among many other things, complaints that the officer forced female inmates to strip and engage in oral sex with one another while he and a number of male prisoners watched and masturbated. [48]

Wisconsin v. Terrell and *Hammond v. Gordon County,* , the graphic representation of outrageous sexual abuses in many of these cases serves to discursively segregate perpetrators, placing them in a category apart from other officers and distancing them as well from the facilities that had employed them. Attribution of blame for the problem of officer-on-prisoner misconduct seems implicit in the graphic narratives describing these incidents, as well as in the courts' tone when discussing incidents of sexual misconduct. Commonly, the courts called alleged officer/perpetrators "malicious,"[49] and "sadistic,"[50] and referred to their behaviors "wanton,"[51] "morally offensive,"[52] criminal,"[53] "repugnant to the conscience of mankind,"[54] and "beyond the pale."[55]

By the time many rights-based cases related to sexual misconduct reached the courts, the rogue officers who had allegedly perpetrated the abuses had long since been dismissed or had resigned under pressure from the facilities where the incidents had occurred. Additionally, some were facing criminal charges while others had already been tried and convicted on sexual assault and related charges. The suspension, dismissal, or resignation of alleged rogue officers, along with their criminal prosecution not only served to further segregate these "bad apples" but also suggests that the problem of sexual misconduct could be solved through the simple weeding out of anomalous rogue officers who were to blame for the problem.

Although there may have been little doubt about the culpability of officers caught perpetrating acts of sexual misconduct, the attribution of collateral blame inspired some debate. In a number of cases, officials – including wardens and assistant wardens – were alleged to share culpability based on claims that they knew or should have known of the risk posed to prisoners by a particular officer. In general, allegations of this nature suggested that prisoner officials either failed to adequately screen their potential employees or that failed to adequately supervise their staff. Along with correctional officials, states and municipalities were occasionally alleged to share blame when it was alleged that incidents of sexual misconduct implicated policy-level inadequacies. A number of plaintiffs alleged that inadequate or ineffective training of officers with respect to managing the safety of prisoners and responding to institutional sexual assault rendered administrators, policymakers, and entire jurisdictions blameworthy. In, *Daskalea v. District of Columbia and Moore* (2000), for example, it was noted that:

> Uncontradicted evidence at the trial of this case established the routine sexual abuse of women inmates by prison guards at the District of Columbia Jail. The plaintiff, Sunday Daskalea, suffered from a continuing course of such abuse, culminating in an evening during which officers forced her to dance naked on a table before more than a hundred chanting, jeering guards and inmates. The District asks us to relieve it of all responsibility for this conduct, contending that the facts fail to establish the "deliberate indifference" necessary to sustain a municipality's liability for the acts of its employees. But deliberate indifference is precisely how any reasonable person would describe the District's attitude toward its women prisoners ...[56]

Although there appears to have been little doubt that rogue officers who perpetrated acts of sexual misconduct were to blame for the problem, not every case was based on allegations that were so clear cut. As discussed earlier in this chapter, a number of prisoners brought charges alleging at least plausible incidents of sexual abuse that occurred within the context of what otherwise amounted to standard, day-to-day prison operations. In the case of *Buckley v. Dallas County*, et al. (2000), for example, the plaintiff alleged that an officer "fondled his genitals in an erotic manner" during the course of a routine pat-down search.[57] As the court's opinion suggests, whether or not the officer could be understood as blameworthy hinged on whether the plaintiff was, in fact, "searched" or whether he was "fondled in an erotic manner." Because many of the "routine procedures" performed by officers were so physically invasive, the distinction between the two had more to do with intent than with a discernable difference in the physical act itself. Ironically, in these cases, the nature of the act and blame for the act became contingent on the intent of the officers performed it. As the following example illustrates, the assignation of blame, therefore, generally became a matter of the plaintiff's word regarding what s/he experienced versus the word of correctional officers about what they intended to do:

> For the subjective element of the test, Buckley must show that the prison guards who allegedly assaulted him did so with a sufficiently culpable state of mind. Defendants Dockery and Hyder have submitted competent summary judgment evidence, in the form of sworn affidavits that the pat-down searches were conducted in a routine and professional manner. The defendants do not specifically remember searching Buckley, but declare that jail policy requires them to search inmates for contraband any time the inmate leaves or returns to the "tank". The search includes touching the area between the inmate's legs to check for hidden contraband. Both defendants state that any search performed on Buckley was conducted systematically and in the manner in which they were instructed....By their affidavits, the defendants negate...Buckley's Eighth Amendment claim and make a prima facie showing of their entitlement to summary judgment.[58]

Taken as a whole, analysis of the data revealed more than one noteworthy finding with regard to how blame for prison sexual violence was assigned in the contemporary era. Most importantly, the attribution of blame in cases deploying a prisoner-on-prisoner assault script stands in sharp contrast to the placement of blame in cases deploying a sexual misconduct script. By the contemporary era, specific "types" of perpetrators had ceased to be blamed for the problem of prisoner-on-prisoner sexual assaults. Rendered discursively as "harm" and understood as violence, prisoner-on-prisoner rape had become a part of the risk that correctional personnel were expected to effectively manage. Thus, at the end of the day, the blame for prisoner-on-prisoner rape was assigned to correctional personnel who failed to successfully manage the risk it posed, not to those who perpetrated it. In contrast, the blame in cases of sexual misconduct was assigned first and foremost to "types" of officers – that is, those anomalous rogue officer or "bad apples" who abused their power over prisoners for their own perverse pleasures and sexual gratification. While there was no small amount of discussion in the courts over the assignment of collateral blame, it was clear that the primary focus was on the perpetrators and, to a much lesser degree, on superior officers, officials, administrators, policymakers, and/or jurisdictions responsible for anticipating and managing the risk these "bad apples" posed to prisoners.

---

[1] 42 U.S.C. § 1997.

[2] A consent decree has the same effect as a judgment at law. Outside the context of the PLRA, consent decrees are considered absolutely binding on the consenting parties and cannot be reviewed *except on a showing that consent was obtained by fraud or that the decree was based on mutual error or the absence consent.*

[3] Total opinions published annually in 2004 = 5; in 2005=10; in 2006=18. Notably, the rapid increase in cases about prison rape heard during these three years followed passage of the Prison Rape Elimination Act in 2003, an event which generated an increased level of awareness of the problem.

[4] http://www.wcl.american.edu/nic/For_Correctional_Employees_Final/ Resolutions/ ACA_Draft_Resolution_%20Staff_Sexual_Misconduct.doc?rd=1 (last visited 07/13/08).

[5] See Chapter 3 for a more detailed description of the extent to which various departments of corrections were named as defendants in litigation of this nature.

[6] The modern debate over "cruel and unusual punishment" commenced with two U.S. Supreme Court cases, *Wilkerson v. Utah* (1878) and *Weems v. United States* (1910). In the former, the Court held that sentences that entail torture and other unnecessary cruelty would violate the Eighth Amendment and in the latter case it broadened the definition of "cruel and unusual punishment" as it tried to balance the proportion of punishment to the crime committed.

[7] *Louisiana ex rel. Francis v. Resweber,* 329 U.S. 459 (1947).

[8] *Estelle v. Gamble,* 429 U.S. 97 (1976).

[9] *Wilson v. Seiter,* 501 U.S. 294 (1991).

[10] http://www.spr.org/en/docs/doc_01_laws.asp (last visited: 07/09/2008).

[11] *Little v. Shelby County,* U.S. Dist. LEXIS 22741 (2000).

[12] Ibid.

[13] "'TENS' is the acronym for Transcutaneous Electrical Nerve Stimulation. A 'TENS unit' is a pocket size, portable, battery-operated device that sends electrical impulses to certain parts of the body to block pain signals." [http://arthritis.about.com/od/assistivedevicesgadgets/g/tensunit.htm, last visited on 01/01/2009].

[14] *Pulliam v. Shelby County,* 902 F. Supp. 797; 1995 U.S. Dist. LEXIS 15082.

[15] *Kemner v. Hemphill,* 199 F. Supp. 2d 1264; 2002 U.S. Dist. LEXIS 9787 (2002).

[16] Ibid.

[17] *Wilson v. Wright, et al.,* 998 F. Supp. 650; 1998 U.S. Dist. LEXIS 3395 (1998).

[18] Ibid.

[19] Ibid.

[20] *Farmer v, Brennan,* 511 U.S. 825; 1994 U.S. LEXIS 4274 (1994).

[21] See *People v. Lovercamp,* 43 Cal. App. 3d 823; 1974 Cal. App. LEXIS 1359 (1974). It should also be noted that this 1974 opinion was the single case in which female prisoners were represented as perpetrators of a sexual assault behind carceral walls.

[22] *Buckley v. Dallas County, et al.,* 2000 U.S. Dist. LEXIS 5543.

[23] Ibid.

[24] *Webb v. Forman,* 1996 U.S. Dist. LEXIS 15227 (1996).

[25] *Rodriguez v. McClenning,* 399 F. Supp. 2d 228; 2005 U.S. Dist. LEXIS 6925 (2005).

[26] *Bromell v. Idaho Department of Corrections, C/O Larry M. Kyle,* 2006 U.S. Dist. LEXIS 80804 (2006).

[27] *Evans and Jordan v. City of Zebulon, Loomis and Stephens,* 351 F.3d 485; 2003 U.S. App. LEXIS 23479; 17 Fla. L. Weekly Fed. C 53 (2003).

[28] *Young v. Poff, et al.,* U.S. Dist. LEXIS (2006).

[29] *Nelson v. Michalko,* 35 F. Supp. 2d 289; 1999 U.S. Dist. LEXIS 880 (1999).

[30] *Styles v. McGinnis et al.,* 28 Fed. Appx. 362; 2001 U.S. App. LEXIS 27314 (2001).

---

[31] It is interesting to note that the courts understood the trauma constituted by cross-gender body searches differently depending on the gender of the "searcher" and "searchee." As the court noted in *Jordan* (1993):

> We are satisfied that the constitutional standard for a finding of sufficient "pain" has been met in this case….[I]n Grummett v. Rushen, 779 F.2d 491 (9th Cir. 1985) this court considered the constitutionality of pat searches performed by female guards on male prisoners. We concluded that the inmates had not shown sufficient evidence of pain to make a cognizable Eighth Amendment claim. Nothing in Gurmmett indicates that men have particular vulnerabilities that would cause the cross-gender clothed body searches to exacerbate symptoms of pre-existing mental conditions. Indeed, in contrast to this case, nothing in Grummett indicates that male prisoners…would be likely to experience any psychological trauma as a result of the searches. The record in this case supports the postulate that women experience unwanted intimate touching by men differently from men subject to comparable touching by women. Several witnesses, including experts in psychology and anthropology, discussed how the differences in gender socialization would lead to differences in the experiences of men and women with regard to sexuality.

[32] *Jordan; Bagley; Hanson; Entz; Wood v. Gardiner et al.*, 986 F.2d 1521 ; 1993 U.S. App. LEXIS 3065 (1993).

[33] Ibid.

[34] *Boddie v. Schneider*, et al., 105 F.3d 857; 1997 U.S. App. LEXIS 1768 (1997).

[35] *White v. Ottinger, et al.*, 442 F. Supp. 2d 236; 2006 U.S. Dist. LEXIS 55243.

[36] *Doe v. Scroggy et al.*, 2006 U.S. Dist. LEXIS 77281 (2006).

[37] *Cain v. Rock and Anne Arundel County*, 67 F. Supp. 2d 544; 1999 U.S. Dist. LEXIS 15880 (1999).

[38] *Szydlowski et al. v. Ohio Department of Rehabilitation and Correction*, 79 Ohio App. 3d 303; 607 N.E.2d 103; 1992 Ohio App. LEXIS 2147 (1992).

[39] Ibid.

[40] *Schwenk v. Hartford*, 204 F.3d 1187 (2000).

[41] *Wilson v. Wright, et al.*, 998 F. Supp. 650 (1998); 1998 U.S. Dist. LEXIS 3395.

[42] *Webb v. Lawrence County*, South Dakota, 144 F.3d 1131; 1998 U.S. App. LEXIS 9607.

[43] Ibid.

[44] *Spruce v. Sargent, et al.*, 149 F.3d 783 ; 1998 U.S. App. LEXIS 15134 (1998).

[45] Ibid.

[46] *Boddie v. Schneider et al.*, 105 F.3d 857 ; 1997 U.S. App. LEXIS 1768.

[47] *Wisconsin v. Terrell*, 2006 WI App 166; 295 Wis. 2d 619 (2006); 2006 Wisc. App. LEXIS 637.

[48] Hammond et al., 316 F. Supp. 2d 1262; 2002 U.S. Dist. LEXIS 27410.

[49] *Doe v. Scroggy, et al.*, 2006 U.S. Dist. LEXIS 77285.

[50] *Wisconsin v. Terrell*, 2006 WI App 166; 295 Wis. 2d 619 (2006); 2006 Wisc. App. LEXIS 637.

[51] *Heckenlaible v. Virginia Regional Penninsula Jail Authority*, 2006 U.S. Dist. LEXIS 53709.

[52] *Hammond et al. v. Gordon County, et al.*, 316 F. Supp. 2d 1262; 2002 U.S. Dist. LEXIS 27410.

[53] Ibid.

[54] *Bromwell v. Idaho Department of Corrections*, 2006 U.S. Dist. LEXIS 80804.

[55] *Boxer X v. Harris*, 49 F. 3d 1114; 2006 U.S. App. LEXIS 20396.

[56] *Daskalea v. District of Columbia and Moore*, 343 U.S. App. D.C. 261; 227 F.3d 433 (2000); 2000 U.S. App. LEXIS 18961.

[57] *Buckley v. Dallas County, et al.*, 2000 U.S. Dist. LEXIS 5543

[58] Ibid..

CHAPTER SIX

Summary and Conclusions

"Prisons are necessarily dangerous places; they house society's most antisocial and violent people in close proximity with one another. Regrettably, '[s]ome level of brutality and sexual aggression among [prisoners] is inevitable no matter what the guards do...unless all prisoners are locked in their cells 24 hours a day and sedated.'"

--Justice Clarence Thomas[1]

THE HISTORICAL ERA

As noted in Chapter Four, by the 1960s, recognition that U.S. prison systems were failing to meet its objectives to protect the public, reduce crime, and rehabilitate offenders was firmly established in the public consciousness. The wave of violence, riots, and prison escapes that plagued carceral facilities across the country during the preceding decade was widely interpreted as signifying that the U.S. penal system was spiraling out of control. Increasing media exposure of the nightmare world inside prison walls, coupled with almost daily reports of rising recidivism rates among released offenders, convinced many of the need for state intervention to remedy the widespread inadequacies of American corrections.

As part of an increase in public discourse about crime and punishment in general – and about violence occurring at correctional facilities across the nation in particular – the subject of prison rape emerged in elite and popular U.S. newspapers in 1969. At least initially, the subject was overwhelmingly framed within a broader discourse about institutional failure – specifically the failure of a U.S.

correctional system that was widely perceived to be out of control and sorely in need of reform. Indeed, more than 80% of the articles published in the historical era framed prison rape in these terms. Having framed the subject in this way, the press deployed a number of related scripts representing the phenomenon not only as a symptom of the prison systems' general failure as an institution, but also of its more specific failure along a number of critical dimensions of correctional performance, including the duties to control prisoners, to rehabilitate them, and to protect the safety of the community outside prison walls. In general, during this time period, the press portrayed U.S. penal institutions as "monster-producing factories," [2] and "schools for crime"[3] where "correction is out of the question" [4] and "rehabilitation programs…nonexistent." [5] In addition to these parallel-running discourses about institutional failure published in the print news media, a lesser number of news articles published during this period employed entirely different, frames to discuss the issue of prison rape. Specifically, a number of articles published prior to 1992 framed prison rape in terms of correctional success – specifically its success as a crime deterrent – and another few historical era articles framed the phenomenon as a myth or, at the very least, an exaggeration.

Not surprisingly in light of the diagnostic frames employed by the historical era press, a majority of articles published during this period pointed the finger of blame at a failing U.S. correctional system. Among the articles that framed blame for prison rape in these terms, most deployed scripts assigning blame to an antiquated, overcrowded, and/or understaffed system that was sorely in need of reform. While a handful of articles attributed part of the blame to negligent or apathetic correctional officers, in general these individuals were seen as "fall guys" for a system that was spiraling out of control and which, at the end of the day, was understood as unmanageable in its current form. Interestingly, as noted in Chapter Two, in conjunction with scripts that attributed blame to the failing correctional system and to violent and incorrigible prisoners, a number of articles deployed a script assigning at least part of the blame for the problem of prison rape to an ignorant or apathetic American public – a public that was either unaware of the problem or alternatively, was aware of it and simply did not care what happened to incarcerated individuals.

In addition to assigning blame for the problem to the failing correctional system and to a lesser degree to the public at large, a significant number of articles published in historical era newspapers blamed particular "types" of prisoners. While other print news media outlets had been addressing the problem of prison rape for some time prior – and in that context frequently blamed "homosexuals" for the problem of prison rape – by the time prison rape was introduced to the newspaper-reading public in 1969, discourse attributing blame for prison rape to types of prisoners had begun to change. By the late 1960s and early 1970s it was not so much "homosexuals" as "homosexuality" that was understood as the issue at the root of the problem of carceral sexual assaults. The difference between the two constructions is significant. While earlier print media outlets had associated prison rape with a type of prisoner (the "homosexual") who brought perverse sexual practices into the carceral environment from outside, by the time the topic of prison rape emerged in U.S. newspapers, sexual perversion in prison had come to associated with violence, uncontrollability, and incorrigibility in general, not with a particular sexual identity. While 43% of the articles published in the historical era attributed blame for the problem to "homosexuality," the attribution referred to a species of problematic prisoners whose behaviors the system was failing to control, not to "homosexuals" *per se*.

The majority of U.S. newspaper articles during this period served more to "discover" prison rape as a social problem for the news-reading public and to attribute blame for it to a generalized "failing system" and to the "incorrigible inmates" it housed than to offer any indication about what could, should, or would be done to address it. Indeed, the vast majority of articles published during this time period offer no inkling whatsoever as to what the solution to the problem might be. Interestingly, however, with the possible exception of articles that framed prison rape as an effective crime deterrent, the various frames and scripts employed and deployed in discovering and assigning blame for prison rape during the historical period may be understood as mutually constitutive. Together, they tell a fairly coherent tale of a prison system perceived as failing, of prison rape as a glaring symptom of that failure, and taken as a whole, they may be understood to pave the way for, help make sense of, and stir public support for the rise of the just deserts model of criminal justice and the large-scale prison buildup that occurred in 1990s and following the turn of the century.

Alongside the discussion of the subject in the historical era print news media, between 1969 and 1991 the appellate courts were generating a variety of identifiable discourses about prison rape. Diagnostic frames employed ranged from representations of prison rape as a crime to prison rape framed as a sentencing factor to prison rape framed as a symptom of institutional failure to prison rape framed as a rights issue. At least in terms of sheer volume, prison rape framed as a crime dominated the discourse in the appellate courts during this era, with more than 25% of the opinions published between 1969 and 1991 framing prison rape in these terms.

As noted in Chapter Four, although prison rape was not "discovered" by the U.S. print news media until 1969, the courts had been dealing with sexual assault behind bars as a prosecutable offense for some time prior to that year. Indeed, "crimes against nature" and "sodomy" perpetrated behind carceral walls were prosecuted in U.S. courts as early as 1915. The year 1969, along with the remainder of the historical era, found the courts still very much engaged in the prosecution of sexual acts between men behind bars. Surprisingly or not given the volume of discourse along these lines generated in the courts, this discourse was not mirrored in contemporaneously published news articles. Nor, in fact, was the discourse that framed prison rape as a sentencing factor in the context of otherwise unrelated criminal trials. Indeed, each of these two frames seems to have been peculiar to the legal arena, with no reference at all made to prison rape in these terms in the contemporary press.

In contrast, much of the discussion of prison rape in the historical era courts mirrored contemporaneously published discourse in the press, framing the phenomenon as a signifier of institutional failure – again, the failure of the U.S. correctional system. The succession of seven escape cases beginning with *People v. Richards* (1969) and ending five years later with *People v. Lovercamp* (1974) embodied this discourse in the historical era courts. Loath to intervene in the business of corrections on both practical and doctrinal grounds, yet increasingly uncomfortable with what it perceived to be an immoral, abusive, and failing institution, in *Lovercamp* the court handed down a decision that was both practically meaningful (albeit a limited sense) and symbolically profound, while at the same time remaining within even most strictly defined limits of judicial power. The court's holding in the case added the threat of rape to the list of circumstances that could constitute a viable defense to charges of escape. More than two-hundred years prior to *Lovercamp,* another court had written in 1 Hale P.C. 611 (1736) that if a prisoner fled from a burning prison, the necessity to save his life "excuseth the felony." With the holding in *Lovercamp,* the list of circumstances that might necessitate escape yet "excuseth the felony" doubled to include both the threat of imminent death *and* the threat of sexual assault as well. The real impact of the well publicized case of *Lovercamp* may be in its symbolic implications. Almost by definition, the fundamental task of a prison is to maintain an impermeable boundary between those "inside" and the community at large. Whatever prisons' remaining functions, they arguably depend on, flow from, or are secondary to the security of its walls. In light of this, the implications of the court's holding in *Lovercamp* seem profound in that, at its core, the decision declared that corrections' failure to provide protection from the imminent threat of rape constituted a legal excuse for prisoners to breach the walls which, in essence, define the institution and protect the community from the felons it contains.

As noted in Chapter Four, in the historical era, the line separating appellate-level legal discourse framing prison rape in terms of institutional failure and that which framed the phenomenon as a rights issue was fuzzy at best. Indeed, as the data revealed, opinions that framed prison rape principally as an indication of correctional failure clearly relied on a discourse of constitutional rights and, likewise, cases framing prison rape primarily as a rights issue also drew on a discourse about institutional failure. Thus, the two discourses told similar stories a prison system which, in its disarray, was infringing on the constitutional rights of the "citizens" it held in captivity. What is perhaps most notable about the legal discourse on the subject is its evolution over time. While high-profile opinions in earlier cases like *Holt v. Sarver I* (1969) and *Holt v. Sarver II* (1970) focused on a whole litany of abuses that rendered entire prison systems unconstitutional, by the middle of the historical era cases tended to be far more focused on the constitutional rights of individual prisoners or small groups of prisoners. Indeed, by the end of the historical era, cases in which the judiciary wielded its injunctive powers with broad sweeping strokes had virtually disappeared, to be largely replaced by cases that awarded monetary damages to individual (and small groups of) plaintiff prisoners.

In general, the data indicated that the historical era courts were somewhat divided in terms of their attribution of blame for the problem of prison rape. On one hand, earlier courts in particular blamed the failing correctional system for the problem. Almost 70% of the opinions published during this period placed blame for the problem at the door of a fundamentally unsound prison system that was unable to maintain a minimum standard of safety for the prisoners in its charge. Over time, however, this discourse came to be challenged by opinions attributing blame for prison rape to individual or small groups of careless or malevolent correctional personnel. Increasingly these "bad apples" were understood to be at fault for failing to protect vulnerable prisoners from sexual assault. Indeed, the discourse assigning blame for the problem to "bad apples" nearly equally that blaming a rotten prison system as a whole. The former attribution, however, tended to characterize discourse produced toward the end of the period, while the latter was more common among opinions published during the earlier years of the historical era, at which time the courts were still very much engaged in their hands-on experiment in prison reform.

Alongside the discourse blaming corrections and correctional personnel, it must be noted that, like the historical era press, the courts blamed particular types of prisoners for the problem of prison rape. Also like the press, the courts blamed those particularly violent and incorrigible prisoners who practiced "homosexuality" first and foremost. In general, the term homosexual was used primarily in adjectival form describing a type of violent behavior – not so much to identify individuals' psycho-sexual identity. Thus, the courts and the press tended to be very much in agreement about what the practice of homosexuality in prison meant. Also like the press, the courts referenced homosexuality with less frequency. While the notion that "homosexuality" was the culprit at fault for the problem of prison rape certainly dominated the discourse early in the historical era, by the latter half of the period, only 30% of the opinions published included such a reference.

THE CONTEMPORARY ERA

In the late 1980s and early 1990s, as the nation shifted toward the political right, the just deserts model of criminal justice was on the rise and the number of persons held in federal, state, and local carceral facilities began to increase dramatically. In conjunction with this changes, discourse about prison rape in the contemporary era press began to shift as well. The framing of prison rape as a symptom of a failing, malevolent, and dysfunctional U.S. correctional system literally disappeared from the discourse in the 1990s as the contemporary era press increasingly came to frame prison rape in new and altered ways.

In the contemporary era print news media, articles discussing prison rape framed the problem first and foremost as a rights-related problem. Although this way of framing sexual violence in prison was not uncommon in the courts in the preceding period, it amounted to a new representation of the phenomenon in the press. The debut of this frame in the early years of the contemporary era is likely attributable to the press's interest in the sudden torrent of prisoner-generated litigation that flooded U.S. courtrooms in the early years of the contemporary period. As noted in Chapter Three, prison rape framed as a "rights problem" rapidly became the construction that would dominate the discourse in the print news media during the contemporary era, with more than 50% of the articles published between 1991 and 2006 framing prison rape in these terms.

Articles that relied on a rights frame generally attempted to make sense of carceral sexual assault through the deployment of one or the other of two dominant scripts. Concomitant with the press's interest in – or at least its coverage of – the massive wave of prisoner generated litigation related to prison rape in the courts, particularly during the first half of the contemporary era the press deployed what amounted to a civil rights script, representing carceral sexual assault principally as constitutional tort related to the Eighth Amendment ban on cruel and unusual punishment. Articles that deployed this script rapidly came to focus a skeptical lens on the often sizeable awards of monetary damages to incarcerated felons who allegedly fell victim to sexual assault in prison. In general, the data suggested that, at an historical moment characterized by extraordinarily high crime rates and a punitive social mood (as witness the series of Ann Landers letters published during the early years of this period), the courts' occupation with prisoners' rights and the awards of monetary damages to those whose rights were impinged did not sit well with the press.

While the civil rights script was most commonly deployed during the first half of the contemporary era, in the latter years of the 1990s and particularly following the turn of the century, articles increasingly came to deploy a human rights script in discussing prison rape. Emerging alongside the civil rights script but ultimately nearly eclipsing it entirely, the human rights script, once it emerged, rapidly came to dominate the discourse about prison rape in the elite and popular print news media. As noted previously, news reports that deployed a human rights script commonly took the form of exposés, offering gritty accounts of the psychological horror and physical trauma associated with prison rape. The emergence and rapid expansion of this script were coincident with the growth and success of interest/human rights groups, the aims of which were, at their core, to generate popular and political interest in favor of a large-scale state response or "solution" to the problem of prison rape. It is interesting to note that the success of these organizations was significant enough that, over time, discourse generated by political actors not only drew upon this human rights discourse but became almost indistinguishable from it. Indeed, as a result of highly successful efforts by human and prisoners' rights groups to place prison rape on the public agenda, growing dissatisfaction with the judicial response to the problem, and increased publicity around corrections' utter lack of response to it, the late 1990s began to witness a dramatic shift in the discourse. Indeed, by the latter years of the decade, discourse in the press had begun to coalesce in favor of a large-scale legislative response to what was increasingly coming to be represented as a critical human rights issue.

By the turn of the last century, the construction of prison rape as a national human rights scandal was commonplace in the American press. Article after article on the subject appeared in elite and popular newspapers published around the country. Indeed, the turn of the century saw the number of news reports on the subject more than double in volume – and in the context of these articles, the call for governmental intervention to address the problem was virtually unanimous and support for new legislation designed to "reduce" or "eliminate" prison rape was nearly universal. Prison rape came to be represented as a national shame and the press all but demanded a response at the national level.

Alongside articles employing a rights frame and deploying either a civil or human rights script, nearly one third of the newspaper articles published in the contemporary era framed prison rape as a crime. In sharp contrast to the legal discourse framing prison rape as a crime against nature (sodomy) during the preceding era, articles in the press that employed a crime frame introduced an entirely new perspective on prison rape. Specifically, the contemporary era press introduced the newspaper-reading public to a staff-on-prisoner sexual misconduct script. While staff-on-prisoner sexual interaction had neither been illegal nor criminal in many jurisdictions until the latter decades of the 20th century, during the first half of the 1990s, federal and state legislatures increasingly passed laws that made sexual misconduct by correctional staff either a felony or at least a misdemeanor. In large part, the deployment of the sexual misconduct script occurred in the context of articles reporting on the arrest, trial, and sentencing of officers accused or convicted of this newly legislated infraction of state and federal laws.

Not only did this script introduce a new type of crime related to sexual violence in carceral settings but it also introduced entirely new players. Indeed, among news articles that deployed a sexual misconduct script, more than 96% pertained to sexual incidents involving a male officer and a female inmate. Thus, rape in carceral settings increasingly came to resemble rape outside prison walls – at least in terms of the gender of the involved parties. Recalling first that female inmates had virtually never been cast as victims of prison rape in the historical era press, and second, the fact that the press had either ignored or been virtually ignorant of staff-on-prisoner sexual misconduct in any form, this new script marked a significant shift in the discourse. It is essential to note in this context that the sexual misconduct framed as a crime was not a part of the discourse that characterized the contemporary era appellate courts. In general, these cases, which garnered so much attention in the press, rarely rose to the appellate level. Indeed, misconduct that was prosecuted tended to be so blatant and, indeed, so well documented that the defendants most often accepted plea bargains and served reduced sentences rather than going to trial at all. Thus, these types of cases rarely generated legal discourse at the appellate level.

By the contemporary era, the notion that prisoners were to blame for the problem of prison rape had all but disappeared from the discourse in the elite and popular press. The homosexual prisoner had ceased to be cast in the role of prison rapist and, in fact, much was made in the press of the notions that rape in prison as elsewhere was about power and violence not sex and that prison rape was generally perpetrated by "heterosexuals" not "homosexuals." Indeed, by the contemporary era, when they were discussed at all, "homosexual" prisoners were understood to be the weak and inagentive victims of rape, not the perpetrators.

Overwhelmingly, the contemporary era press attributed blame for the problem of prison rape to corrections. This was by no means a continuation of the discourse about a failing correctional system that had dominated discussions in the press during the historical era, however. Indeed, by this time corrections was generally understood to be a sound institution – but at the same time, one with problems. If corrections was understood to be to blame for the problem – and it was – it was not because the entire institution was dysfunctional. Instead, corrections' blame for prison rape was represented in the contemporary era press in two related ways - either as a manifestation of a problematic institutional culture or, alternatively, as problem related to staffing – specifically, the failure to control or eliminate "rogue officers" or "bad apples" among the ranks of correctional staff. Overall, these scripts were each associated with particular diagnostic frames and scripts. That is, articles that deployed a human rights script tended to blame institutional culture for the problem, which articles deploying a constitutional rights script of framing prison rape as a crime tended to blame rogue officers among the ranks.

Finally, as was the case in the historical era, a relatively small portion of contemporary-era news articles blamed the public for the problem of prison rape. However, it should also be noted that while articles directly blaming public indifference constituted a relatively minor discourse, over time an increasing number of news articles on prison rape – in particular those that framed the problem as a human rights issue – seem intended to speak directly to the public with the intent to stir popular concern. Particularly around the turn of the last century, as the discourse began to coalesce in favor of a legislative response to the problem, the voice of human rights in the press seems increasingly to have been aimed at mobilizing an indifferent and apathetic public.

While the discourse about prison rape in the contemporary era press increasingly came to coalesce around a human rights discourse, the breadth of the discourse on the subject in the appellate courts narrowed as well. After 1991, the cases that came before the appellate courts increasingly represented prison rape and other forms of carceral sexual violence in the language of Eighth Amendment jurisprudence and accordingly, the subject came to be framed almost exclusively as "harm." However, the nature and extent of the harm constituted by carceral sexual violence varied considerably in accordance with the script deployed in specific cases.

As was the case with news articles published after 1991, the most notable shifts in legal discourse that occurred in the contemporary era pertained to the gender of prison rape victims and the introduction of the sexual misconduct script. While only one pre-1991 case deployed a sexual misconduct script, in the contemporary era cases deploying that script constituted the modal category. Concomitant with the glut of cases related to staff-on-prisoner sexual abuse after 1991 was an equally dramatic increase in the number of opinions related to claims involving female prisoners – specifically, female prisoners who were victims of staff sexual misconduct. In the contemporary era, about 43% of contemporary era cases deploying a sexual misconduct script pertained to female victims.

Analysis of the data indicated that cases of "prisoner-on-prisoner assault" differed markedly from cases of "sexual misconduct" in these terms. Opinions that deployed a "prisoner-on-prisoner assault" script were notable first and foremost for the extreme violence that characterized the discourse on the subject in the appellate courts. In these opinions, the "harm" of prison rape was constituted by the corporal violence associated with these acts, along with their attendant psychological and spiritual manifestations. In contrast, while coercion was generally explicit in cases of sexual misconduct and violence implicit, opinions that deployed a sexual misconduct script generally represented the harm associated with this type of assault as an abuse of power rather than as violence per se. Interestingly, in many opinions in the latter category – in particular those associated with sexual abuse of female prisoners by male officers – the discourse drew on a vocabulary generally associated with perverse sensuality and romantic relationships rather than the lexicon of violence that characterized the courts' discourse about prisoner-on-prisoner assaults. At the end of the day, the impression left in these cases was that male-on-female abuse in carceral settings closely mirrored sexualized harassment and abuses of women by men that occur daily outside prison walls, while the abuse of male prisoners, regardless of the gender of the perpetrator, was represented as violence.

As was the case with news media discourse in the contemporary era, by this time the courts had largely ceased to blame "types" of prisoners for the problem of prison rape. The rise and generalized acceptance of the just deserts model of criminal justice had placed prison officials back in control of prisons and thus – as was the case in the contemporary media – the courts had increasingly come to place blame for the ongoing problem of prison rape at the door of corrections.

The assignation of blame for the harm of prison rape, however, was by no means uniform across scripts, despite the fact that the finger was generally pointed in the same direction – at correctional officers. Indeed, blame in cases of sexual misconduct was understood quite differently from blame in cases of prisoner-on-prisoner assault.

Like the contemporary era print news media, in cases involving staff-on-prisoner sexual misconduct, the discourse generated in the appellate courts placed the blame for prison rape largely on the shoulders of individual rogue officers or "bad apples" who, acting outside the parameters of their official duties, sexually abused the prisoners in their charge. The courts left little doubt as to their opinion of these "bad apples," calling them "malicious,"[6] and "sadistic;"[7] "wanton,"[8] "morally offensive,"[9] criminal,"[10] "repugnant.[11] As noted in Chapter Five, by the time many cases related to sexual misconduct reached the courts, the "bad apples" who had allegedly perpetrated the abuses had either been dismissed or resigned from their employment at the facilities where the incidents had occurred. Many faced criminal charges stemming from their misconduct. The suspension, dismissal, or resignation of these rogue officers served to effectively divorce "bad apples" from the correctional system that had employed them and, in addition, served as an indication that the problem of sexual misconduct could be solved through weeding out anomalous rogue officers. Thus, while collateral blame was occasionally placed at the door of prison administrators, other officers, or the prison system itself, in general its was the bad apples who were understood as blameworthy.

In terms of assigning blame for prisoner-on-prisoner sexual violence – when blame was indeed assigned at all – the courts almost uniformly pointed the finger at the correctional officers charged with managing the pervasive risk of violence which, by now, was widely understood to be inherent in the carceral environment. However, recalling what was made clear in Chapter Five – specifically that where intent on the part of officers was not demonstrable, sexual violence was rendered constitutionally irrelevant – in many of the cases heard by the appellate courts in the contemporary era, blame for the problem was, in essence, rendered irrelevant as well. Thus, where the high standard the Court established to show that officers acted with a sufficiently culpable state of mind was not met, prison rape became an unintentional hazard of living in a carceral environment. As Justice Thomas remarked in his concurring opinion in *Farmer v. Brennan* (1994), "Prisons are necessarily dangerous places; they house society's most antisocial and violent people in close proximity with one another. Regrettably, '[s]ome level of brutality and sexual aggression among [prisoners] is inevitable no matter what the guards do...unless all prisoners are locked in their cells 24 hours a day and sedated.'"[12]

The standard of proof established by the Court in *Farmer* led to a disjuncture between "common-sense" attributions of blame based on the legal narratives and the ultimate legal outcomes in the appellate courts. Although prisoner-on-prisoner rape narratives often left little doubt that correctional officers were to blame, the inability of the court to assign blame where logic suggests it clearly belonged seems to almost to defy common sense. The disjuncture between the logical implications of the narrative and the contradictory legal outcomes suggests that the framing of prison rape as an Eighth Amendment rights issue may not have been the most advantageous approach in terms of achieving justice for victims of prisoner-on-prisoner violence. Further, as close reading of the data indicated and as others have noted, the standard for attributing legal blame in the context of the Eighth Amendment was applied unevenly, leading to entirely different outcomes in cases that read as factually identical.[13]

Taken as a whole, the data from this analysis offered an opportunity to map the trajectory of thought about prison rape in the United States' appellate courts and print news media over the course of the 38-year period prior to and immediately following legislative action that led to passage of the Prison Rape Elimination Act (2003). Tracing the frames employed to discuss the subject and the scripts deployed to make sense of and respond to it, the data analyzed shed significant light on the making of meaning in each of these two important arenas of public discourse, the relationship between them, and how that relationship did and did not change over time.

As the preceding analysis indicated, the story told by the data suggests that the meaning of prison rape in each of these two social locations was initially nearly identical and over the course of the historical era, changes in one arena were generally reflected in the other. As prison rape morphed over time from perversion to punishment in both arenas, in each, blame for the problem was assigned almost uniformly to a prison system that was widely understood to be rotten at its core. Over time, however, the discourse generated in each of these social locations began to diverge such that, by the middle of the contemporary era, the two had taken quite different paths.

Largely as a result of the efforts of various interest groups such as Stop Prisoner Rape, Prison Fellowship Ministries, Human Rights Watch, and various groups working under the auspices of the United Nations, contemporary era media discourse on the subject began to reflect a human rights perspective. While the discourse of the press cannot be understood to constitute popular consciousness, it does help to shape it and, over time, the discourse of human rights did in fact come to dominate *public* discussion of the subject.

In contrast, while the courts may have played the role of reformer in the historical era as they wielded their power of judicial injunction with broad strokes, by the middle of the contemporary era, their ability dispense justice for individual prison rape victims was becoming increasingly clear. Recognizing on one hand that prison rape was part and parcel of the penal environment, on the other the courts almost universally blamed rogue officers for the problem. While the courts were effective in the sense that they did prosecute the "crime" of sexual misconduct and frequently imprisoned the "bad apples" that sullied the good name of correctional officers, their inability to address the pervasive problem of sexual violence in U.S. prisons was increasingly apparent. At the end of the day, it remained for the legislature – in fact the very branch of government that many had expected to address the problem prior to the courts' reluctant intervention in penal matters many decades prior – to begin to address anew the problem of epidemic sexual abuse in U.S. prisons.

---

[1] *Farmer v. Brennan*, 511 U.S. 825 (1994).

[2] "*De Profundis.*" *The Register*, Danville, Virginia. April 4, 1969.

[3] "Crisis in the Prisons: Not Enough Room for All the Criminals." *U.S. News and World Report*. November 28, 1977.

[4] "*De Profundis*." *The Register*, Danville, Virginia. April 4, 1969.

[5] "Administration Terms Report 'Sensational.'" *The Pharos-Tribune & Press*, Logansport, Indiana. March 26, 1969.

[6] *Doe v. Scroggy, et al.*, 2006 U.S. Dist. LEXIS 77285.

[7] *Wisconsin v. Terrell*, 2006 WI App 166; 295 Wis. 2d 619 (2006); 2006 Wisc. App. LEXIS 637.

[8] *Heckenlaible v. Virginia Regional Peninsula Jail Authority*, 2006 U.S. Dist. LEXIS 53709.

[9] *Hammond et al. v. Gordon County, et al.*, 316 F. Supp. 2d 1262; 2002 U.S. Dist. LEXIS 27410.

[10] Ibid.

[11] *Bromwell v. Idaho Department of Corrections*, 2006 U.S. Dist. LEXIS 80804.

[12] *Farmer v. Brennan*, 511 U.S. 825 (1994)

[13] See (Giller 2004).

References

Albiston, Catherine. 2003. "The Paradox of Losing by Winning: The Rule of Law and the Litigation Process" in Herb Ritzer and Susan Silbey (eds). 2003. *In Litigation: Do the Haves Still Come Out Ahead?* Palo Alto: Stanford University Press.

Austin, James, Tony Fabelo, Angela Gunter, and Ken McGinnis. 2006. "Sexual Violence in the Texas Prison System"(Report submitted to the United States Department of Justice).

Beckett, K. 2001. "Crime and Control in the Culture of Late Modernity" (Review). *Law & Society Review,* 35:4, 899-930.

Benford, Robert D. and David A. Snow. 2000. "Framing Processes and Social Movements: An Overview and Assessment." *Annual Review of Sociology,* 26: 611-639.

Chavez, Linda. "Prison's dirty secrets are being exposed in Congress." *Jewish World Review,* July 2, 2003. http://www.jewishworldreview.com/cols/chavez070203.asp .

Connolly, Catherine. 1998. "An Analysis of Judicial Opinions in Same-Sex Visitation and Adoption Cases." *Behavioral Sciences and the Law,* 14:2, 187-203.

Curtis, Kim. "Disputed study: Rape rare in prisons," Associated Press, January 17, 2006. http://www.spr.org/en/sprnews/2006/0117.asp .

DiMaggio, Paul. 1997. "Culture and Cognition." *Annual Review of Sociology* 23: 263-287.

Fleischer, Mark (2008). *The Myth of Prison Rape: Sexual Culture in American Prisons.* Rowman & Littlefield Publishers, Inc.: Lanham, MD.

Fleisher, Mark S. and Jessie L. Krienert. 2006. "The Culture of Prison Sexual Violence." (Report prepared for the U. S. Department of Justice).

Fogel, David. (1979). *We Are the Living Proof: The Justice Model for Corrections* (2nd ed.). Cincinnati: Anderson Publishing.

Foucault, Michel. 1972. *The Archaeology of Knowledge*. Trans. A. M. Sheridan Smith. New York: Pantheon.

Foucault, Michel. 1976. *Discipline and Punish: The Birth of the Prison*. New York, NY: Vintage Books.

Fuller, Bruce, Susan D. Holloway, Marylee F. Rambaud, and Constanza Eggers-Pierola. 1996. "How Do Mothers Choose Child Care? Alternative Cultural Models in Poor Neighborhoods." *Sociology of Education* 69:83-104.

Gaes, Gerald, G., Scott D. Camp, Julianne B. Nelson, and William G. Saylor. 2004. *Measuring Prison Performance: Government Privatization and Accountability*. Walnut Creek, CA: AltaMira Press.

Gamson, W. A. (1989). "News as Framing." *American Behavioral Scientist*, 33, 157-161..

Gamson, W.A. and A. Modigliani. 1987. "Media Discourse and Public Opinion on Nuclear Power: A Constructionist Approach." *American Journal of Sociology*, 95, 1-37

Garland. David. 1990. "Frameworks of Inquiry in the Sociology of Punishment." *The British Journal of Sociology*, Vol. 41, No. 1 (Mar. 1990), 1-15.

Garland, David. 1991. "Sociological Perspectives on Punishment." *Crime and Justice*, Vol. 14, 115-165.

Garland, David. 2001. *The Culture of Control: Crime and Social Order in Contemporary Society*. New York: Oxford University Press

Garland, David. (2004). "Beyond the Culture of Control." *Critical Review of International Social and Political Philosophy*, Vol. 7, No. 2, 160-89.

Giller, Olga. 2004. "Patriarchy on Lockdown: Deliberate Indifference and Male Prison Rape." 10 *Cardozo Women's Law Journal*, 659.

Goffman, E. 1974. *Frame Analysis*. New York: Harper & Row.

Haas, Kenneth C. 1977. "Judicial Politics and Correctional Reform: An Analysis of the Decline of the 'Hands-Off' Doctrine. *Detroit College of Law Review*: 795, 1977.

Harding, David J. 2006. "Cultural Context, Sexual Behavior, and Romantic Relationships in Disadvantaged Neighborhoods." Research Report 06-612. (Presented to the Population Studies Center, University of Michigan Institute for Social Research).

Holloway, Susan D., Bruce Fuller, Marylee F. Rambaud, and Constanza Eggers-Pierola. 1997. *Through My Own Eyes: Single Mothers and the Cultures of Poverty.* Cambridge, MA: Harvard University Press.

Human Rights Watch. 1996. *All Too Familiar: Sexual Abuse of Women in U.S. State Prisons.* New York: Human Rights Watch.

"Inmate Sexual Assault: An Overview of Selected Print and Electronic Resources." Prepared by Larry Linke. National Institute of Corrections Information Center. October 2002. http://www.nicic.org/pubs/2003/ 018794.pdf. (last visited 12/28/07).

Irwin, John. 1980. *Prisons in Turmoil.* Boston: Little, Brown.

Jenness, Valerie, Cheryl L. Maxson, Kristy N. Matsuda, and Jennifer Macy Sumner. 2007. "Violence in California Correctional Facilities: An Empirical Examination of Sexual Assault." (Report submitted to the California Department of Corrections and Rehabilitation).

Lipton, Douglas, R. Martinson, and J. Woks, *The Effectiveness of Correctional Treatment: A Survey of Treatment Valuation Studies.* New York: Praeger Press.

Lyon, David. 2003. "The Culture of Control: Crime and Social Order in Contemporary Society (Review). *American Journal of Sociology,* Vol 109, No. 1, p. 258.

Martin, J. 1992. *Cultures in Organizations: Three Perspectives.* New York: Oxford University Press.

Otis, Margaret. 1913. "A Perversion Not Commonly Noted," *Journal of Abnormal Psychology* 8:112-16.

Park, James J. (2001). "Redefining Eighth Amendment Punishments: A New Standard for Determining the Liability of Prison Officials for Failing to Protect Inmates from Serious Harm." *Quinnipiac Law Review* (20 QLR 407).

Phillips, Scott and Ryken Grattet. 2000. "Judicial Rhetoric, Meaning-Making, and the Institutionalization of Hate Crime Law." *Law & Society Review,* *Vol. 34,* No. 3, 567-606.

Pinello, Daniel. 2003. *Gay Rights and American Law.* Oxford University Press: New York.

Quinn, Naomi and Dorothy Holland. 1987. "Culture and Cognition." p. 3-40 in Dorothy Holland and Naomi Quinn eds. *Cultural Models in Language and Thought.* Cambridge: Cambridge University Press.

Reports of the Prison Discipline Society of Boston. 1972. (Publication No. 155: Reprint Series in Criminology, Law Enforcement, and Social Problems). Patterson Smith: Montclair, New Jersey.

Richman, Kimberly. 2002. "Lovers and Legal Strangers." *Law & Society Review*, Vol. 36, No. 2, 285-325.

Robertson, James E. 2003. "A Clean Heart and an Empty Head: The Supreme Court and Sexual Terrorism in Prison." *North Carolina Law Review*, Vol. 81: 433-481.

Sacco, Vincent F. 1995. "Media Constructions of Crime" Annals of the American Academy of Political and Social Science, Vol. 539, Reactions to Crime and Violence. Pp. 141-154.

Savelsberg, J.J. (2002). "Cultures of Control in Contemporary Societies." *Law and Social Inquiry*, Vol. 27, No. 3, 685.

Schmierbach, Michael. 2004. *Measuring Media Texts and Understanding Media Effects: A Conceptual and Experimental Examination of News Stories and Cognition*. Dissertation: University of Wisconsin-Madison.

Sewell, William. "The Concept(s) of Culture." p. 35-61 in Victoria E. Bonnell and Lynn Hunt, eds. *Beyond the Cultural Turn*. Berkeley: University of California Press.

Snow, David A., E. Burke Rochford, Jr. Steven K. Worden, and Robert D. Benford. 1986. *American Sociological Review*, 51:464-481.

Sullivan, Larry E. 1990. *The Prison Reform Movement: Forlorn Hope*. Boston: Twayne.

Swidler, Ann. 1986. "Culture in Action: Symbols and Strategies. *American Sociological Review*, 51, 2, 273-286.

Swidler, Ann. 1997. *Talk of Love: How Americans Use Their Culture*. Chicago: University of Chicago Press.

Violence Silence: Why no one really cares about prison rape. Robert Weisberg and David Mills. Posted Wednesday, Oct. 1, 2003, at 2:07 PM ET http://www.slate.com/id/2089095/.

Index

A

Advocate, 36
African Americans, 37–38, 45, 71–72, 86, 115
AIDS, 50, 56–58
Alabama's Habitual Felony Offender Act (1979), 93
Alberti v. Klevenhagen (1985), 106, 109, 120–121
alcohol, 55, 108
Alford, William Lee, 118
All Too Familiar: Sexual Abuse of Women in U.S. State Prisons, 48
Allred Unit, 73–74
American Correctional Association, 67, 131
Andrews, Joe, 64
appellate court, 2, 10–14, 23, 51, 54, 90–94, 112-115, 120, 130, 166, 171-175
Arkansas Democrat-Gazette, 58, 75–76
Arkansas Department of Corrections (ADC), 58
Arkansas State Penitentiary System, 106, 120
Associated Press (AP), 29–30, 55, 59, 73, 76

B

Baldi, (Warden), 34
Barry, Jean, 113
"Behind Those Prison Riots", 20
Belmont Rotary Club, 65
Bilger, Steven, 152

Birmingham News, 59, 60
Black Gangster Disciples Gang, 114
Blackmun, (Justice), 131, 137
blame. *See also* specific groups
    assigning, 164–165, 174–176
    institutional culture, 72–74
    municipalities, 156
    sexual misconduct, 153–158
    shifting attributions, 71–72
    states, 156
    "the system", 31, 119–122
Blucker, Michael Eric, 55, 57, 68, 74
Blucker, Sue, 57
Boddie v. Schneider, et al. (1997), 143, 154
body searches, 142
Boston Globe, 27, 50, 56–57, 58–59, 66–67
Boston Prison Discipline Society, 1
Boyer, Oliver "Glenn", 54
Brewer, Alexander Paul, 91–92
Bromell, Steven, 140–141
Bromell v. Idaho Department of Corrections (2006), 140–141
Buckley v. Dallas County, et al. (2000), 139, 156–157
Buck's County jail, 31–32
Bureau of Prisons, 76
Bush, George W., 1

C

Cahill, Tom, 48
Cain v. Rock and Anne Arundel County (1999), 145–146
California Correctional Training Facility, 100